DAVID BOWIE

The Collector

NICK SMART

McNIDDER & GRACE

Published by McNidder & Grace
21 Bridge Street
Carmarthen SA31 3JS
Wales, United Kingdom

www.mcnidderandgrace.com

First Published 2025

Image credits: front cover © Philippe Auliac; b/w section (between pp.137–144), p.1, top, © Madeline Bocaro, bottom, Mark Plati; p.2, top, Gillian Johnson, bottom Christoper Johnson (https://creativecommons.org//licenses/by-sa/2.0/), p.3, top, © Philippe Auliac. Andy Jones, pp. 3 bottom; 4 top; 5 bottom; 6 top. Kathrine Smart, pp. 4 bottom; 5 top; 6 bottom. Nick Smart, p.2 bottom. Colour plate section: Duffy – Photo Duffy © Duffy Archive, pp.1, 3, 5; © Philippe Auliac pp. 2, 4, 6, 7, 8, 9, 10 top, 11, 12, 13, 14, 15 bottom; Photo © David Currie, 2024. All Rights Reserved (from the book *The Grand Illusion of David Bowie* by David Currie, Legends Publishing 2024), p.15 top; ©Boris Yaro, p.10 bottom; p.16, Helen Green.

A catalogue record for this work is available from the British Library.

ISBN 9780857162786
eISBN 9780857162793

Cover design: Tabitha Palmer, Wales
Designer: JS Typesetting Ltd, Porthcawl, Wales
Printed and bound in the United Kingdom by Short Run Press

An intelligent, knowledgeable and comprehensive look at the world of Bowie through the eyes of the people he worked with.
David Quantick, author, movie writer, television writer and radio broadcaster

Here's Bowie's tale told accurately in the only possible way – by meeting the people involved and asking them exactly what happened.
Joel McIver, author

Over the years, I've met quite a few really good authors, journalists, etc. who know their stuff on David Bowie. Nick Smart is right up there with the best of them. He's also a great bloke and I'm pleased that he has finally put all his knowledge about David into a book. That's why I'm banging the drum for Nick.
John Cambridge, rock drummer and musician

A well-researched dive into the myriad phases of Bowie's creative world, referencing the many musicians and collaborators who helped bring his turbulent visions to studios and stages across five decades of a unique artistic journey that has touched us all.
Kevin Armstrong, guitarist, producer, songwriter

There are scores of books about the legend that is David Bowie which investigates his life, body and soul, but this dives deep into the DNA of a polymath, a performer, a poet and a prophet whose story captivated generations and will continue to enchant for those yet to come.
Robin Morgan, media director

A gripping read and a must for Bowie fans. Packed with intricate, well-researched and little-known detail on the multi-dimensional swirl around Bowie's creative genius.
Victoria Broackes, co-curator of 'David Bowie is' (V&A)

The narrative that Nick Smart has woven throughout The Collector *keeps you moving at top speed through David's ever-changing world. It lays out David's lifelong quest to satisfy his inexhaustible curiosity on a scale that really becomes apparent when taken as a whole; as a participant in a certain period of his evolution, I realize how lucky I was to be involved in even a short portion of his journey. An adventure like no other.*
Mark Plati, musician

This insightful and well-researched look into David Bowie's career and creative process from devoted fan Nick Smart is a welcome addition to the canon of books about his extraordinary life. Filled with details and interviews from the people around him who were there when it happened, it's an informative read about an inspiring man and his process.
Donny McCaslin, saxophonist

For Kathrine, Sophie, Joshua and Sky

FOREWORD

Since 2016, Nick Smart and his co-editor Andy Jones have been producing a splendid fanzine called *David Bowie Glamour*. If you've been fortunate enough to get your hands on a copy or three (and if you haven't, you really must), then you'll know that *David Bowie Glamour* is a true labour of love: a publication which brings together the testimonies of fans and colleagues alike, setting the reminiscences of David's collaborators – fellow musicians, producers, actors, photographers, directors, dancers, designers, promoters – alongside the no less precious memories of devoted fans who were there in the crowd for every step of Bowie's long and colourful career. Lavishly produced and beautifully illustrated, *David Bowie Glamour* has expanded over the years into a rich and invaluable archive – and now Nick Smart has drawn upon these accumulated interviews, encounters and adventures in the Bowie universe to form the basis of the volume you're reading. Tipping his hat to a moment of self-analysis offered up by the great man himself in a celebrated 1973 interview with Russell Harty, Nick has called his book *The Collector* – so it seems entirely apt that the assembled volumes of *David Bowie Glamour* have themselves contributed to a new exploration of David Bowie's lifelong habit of collecting ideas and enthusiasms from the world around him.

Thanks in great measure to his insatiable appetite for the unusual, the unexpected and the avant garde, David Bowie was more than just any old genius: he became a kind of cultural gateway. Bowie was an artist who guided us in the direction of the good stuff, enthusiastically sharing the wonders he had so voraciously gathered around him. Even as we marvelled at his own exceptional body of work, he was opening our minds and educating us, introducing us to new artists, to imaginative possibilities and ways of looking at the world that we might otherwise never have considered. His creative habit of collecting scraps of ideas and influences from cultures high and low, exotic and domestic, familiar and arcane, and then creating something new by recontextualising them all through the prism of his own extraordinary talent: this was a fundamental ingredient of the Bowie magic. To coin a phrase, he opened strange doors that we'd never close again.

The endlessly shifting, creatively restless, multi-disciplinary nature of that five-decade career, the tumbling kaleidoscope of platforms and media through which David Bowie chose to express himself, means that he came to each and every one of us via a slightly different route, a different set of circumstances. This, coupled of course with the small matter of our varying ages, means that we each have our own cherished memories of the seminal moments that drew us into the wonderful world of David Bowie. Mine include hearing the instrumental intro of 'Sound and Vision' used as a sound-bed on BBC television trailers in early 1977, and wondering what this mesmerising jingle was, and whether I could get hold of it (happily, I could – it was the first single I ever bought with my own pocket money); and then, a couple of years later, seeing Bowie perform 'Boys Keep

Swinging' on *The Kenny Everett Video Show* – that David Mallet-directed prototype for the song's official video, shot on a similar set but without the trio of backing singers, Bowie resplendent in a tight black shirt and voluminous trousers, clutching a cigarette as he vamped and sang. The comedy skit at the end, as he struck a sequence of preening poses with his violin while Angry of Mayfair set about him with an umbrella, was great fun, but it was the song itself that reeled me in: those intriguing lyrics about cherries popping and boys checking each other out, snarled into camera by that strange, angular, handsome man, at once funny and sinister, deploying goofy jazz-hands, careening back from the microphone at forty-five degrees while drumming an outstretched leg on the floor with such force that the scenery wobbled. What a bizarre spectacle it was. I was bewitched, and my love affair began in earnest.

Whatever route brought you to David Bowie, and whatever spells he has cast on you over the years, I think you'll agree that one of the greatest gifts of his remarkable legacy is that he continues to bring us all together. In the end, we all belong in David Bowie's collection.

Nicholas Pegg
October 2024

CONTENTS

PREFACE

Carlos Alomar steps onto the stage. What vision is this? His hair is spiked. He wears round glasses with holographic eyes which make him look like a mad, four-eyed insect. His black biker jacket is effortlessly cool and his Kramer guitar is slung around his neck. Known as a rhythm guitarist, he is shredding with the best of them — and the sight is awesome. This moment is magic.

Before long, David Bowie, decked head to toe in red, is lowered to the stage, speaking into a telephone, as he had done during the famous Diamond Dogs shows 13 years previously. Then he's singing, "Gone, gone. The water's all gone / Mummy come back 'cause the water's all gone," and we're all dancing. Seventy thousand of us. Carlos. And Bowie. And all of us. Dancing and thinking only of now.

We spend over two hours thinking only of now.

The next day, we do it all again in a different location. We've made some memories. My uncle, Andy, running into the stadium to secure our preferred spot. My brother Steve, aged 13, crying with emotion after 'Modern Love'. My girlfriend, now wife, buying a portion of chips and finding in it, of all things, the neck of a broken bottle! We have some stories to tell.

It's 1987. The tour will be derided in years to come, and

I do understand why. Some of the intricacies pass us by due to the scale of the arena and our distance – but everyone there on the day had the time of their lives.

I can date my Bowie fandom to three different dates. In 1973, Andy gave me a copy of 'The Jean Genie' b/w 'Ziggy Stardust'. It seemed like a sound from another world. Needless to say, I played it over and over again. Around the same time, I saw the video for 'John, I'm Only Dancing' on TV and similarly had my eyes opened to a strange world that I hadn't considered might exist before. I was six years old. I can't really claim that that was the moment I became a fan.

The second is a school trip in 1979, when I bought three singles with my own money. 'Sunday Girl' by Blondie, 'Boys Keep Swinging' by Bowie and Showaddywaddy's 'Remember Then'. Two out of three.

Closer.

But the real moment was on a family holiday to France in 1980, when I bought *Scary Monsters (and Super Creeps)*. At the age of 13, I was transformed – and hooked. And then I had a three-year wait for the next album. Bowie taught me patience. But, of course, I had a huge back catalogue to discover.

Over the years Andy and I discussed how to escape the routine of everyday life and involve ourselves in the Bowie world more. Andy wanted to buy and sell records and memorabilia. I thought that would be great, too, but I guess I wanted to write. We thought about starting a fanzine. Decades passed. Eventually, in October 2016, I said, "What about this fanzine, then?" It seemed the time was now right. Andy was semi-retired and I was looking for something different. If we'd realised how little we knew about running a magazine, we wouldn't have done it. Luckily, we simply pressed ahead.

And we started an adventure. An adventure that meant that the figure on the stage with the spiky hair and cool glasses became someone we got to know personally, along with his fabulous wife Robin Clark, who sang on *Young Americans* and calls my wife Kathrine her soul sister. In fact, we got to meet and interview many people who were friends and confidants of Bowie.

We also curated two international Bowie conventions. One in Liverpool in 2022 and one in New York the following year. We were able to use the address book we had built up over the years of doing the fanzine to invite a brilliant array of Bowie alumni, including Carlos and Robin, Woody Woodmansey, Donny McCaslin, Gail Ann Dorsey, Tony Visconti, Mark Plati, George Murray, Kevin Armstrong, Tim Palmer, Carmine Rojas and John Cambridge – and the amazing Bowie authority Nicholas Pegg as compère. We were visited by the acclaimed film director Brett Morgen whose sizzling Bowie film *Moonage Daydream* was released in September 2022, and by Victoria Broackes and Geoffrey Marsh, curators of the massively successful 'David Bowie is' exhibition at the V&A. Jonathan Barnbrook, who designed many Bowie record sleeves, was with us. We had a photography exhibition with the Duffy Archive, Denis O'Regan and Philippe Auliac. We had Bowie expert Kevin Cann, academics Bethany Usher and Alex Sharpe and amazing live music from David Live, The London Boys and Rebel Heroes.

It was fabulous. And what a journey from the day that I bought *Scary Monsters* to watching that show in '87, to… all this!

It was then that I began to realise that we had built up a substantial database of interviews from across Bowie's whole career. I'll list just the musicians and producers in order of appearance:

> *Carlos Alomar, Mike Garson, Woody Woodmansey, Tony Visconti, Ian Hunter, Tony Sales, Robin Clark, Catherine Russell, Mark Plati, Kevin Armstrong, Gerry Leonard, Carmine Rojas, Rick Wakeman, Mark Guiliana, Tim Lefebvre, Jason Lindner, Donny McCaslin, Ben Monder, Tim Palmer, Earl Slick, George Murray, Harry Maslin, Eduard Meyer, Reeves Gabrels, Emm Gryner, John Cambridge, Alan Childs, Gail Ann Dorsey, Zack Alford, Sterling Campbell, Peter Noone and Ken Scott.*

That's over 30 musicians and producers. And we have also spoken to many other insiders, and other musicians influenced by Bowie in some way: Joe Elliott, Holly Johnson, Steve Norman, Richard Jobson, Clem Burke, Glen Matlock, Glenn Gregory, Kenney Jones and many more.

It was at this point that I began to feel it would be right to bring all of this together in a book.

INTRODUCTION

Before I started writing this book, I thought I knew a lot about Bowie. In fact, what I knew was the facts of his career. I never met David Bowie, but through getting to know many of his friends, I have learned two things – that as a person he was warm, witty and friendly, not at all the aloof artist I once imagined – and that his genius lay in his ability to collect influences, to rearrange them, interpret them, to set them against each other, and thereby to fashion something entirely new. Ted Hughes once said of his wife, the poet Sylvia Plath, "Her attitude to her verse was artisan-like: if she couldn't get a table out of the material, she was quite happy to get a chair, or even a toy. The end product for her was not so much a successful poem, as something that had temporarily exhausted her ingenuity." So, it seems with Bowie. He would begin to combine, alter, transform both sonically and lyrically, often intentionally not considering what the product will be. The journey determined the outcome. Not always, but often.

That Bowie often changed his musical style and appearance is well-known, of course. Bowie as collector is the subject of this book, and by 1980 he had amassed enough of a back catalogue to begin to borrow from himself.

The first of these changes that the public was aware of

happened in 1974, when Bowie jumped the sinking ship of glam rock with perfect timing and hitched a ride with American funk and plastic soul, waving to those who lacked the foresight to do the same – T. Rex, Sweet, Wizzard and many others who continued with their hitherto successful formulae. These frequent changes of direction did not start in 1974, however. They had been a feature of Bowie's *modus operandi* from the start of his career in 1962. He had been mod, beatnik, hippy, and any number of other images that are less easily labelled. Along with these frequent changes of direction came an equal number of changes of personnel – and it was this relentless pursuit that led to Bowie's reputation for ruthlessness. The curious feature of this tendency to move on and leave old partners behind is that, as Dylan Jones notes, most people didn't seem to feel much animosity as a result. The general feeling was that they'd had their time with Bowie and now things were moving on. By the time success beckoned, Bowie had already left a whole slew of bands: the Konrads, the Hooker Brothers, the King Bees, the Manish Boys, the Lower Third, the Buzz, the Riot Squad, Hype.

But this isn't a book about how David Bowie changed over a period of time. That is already well documented. This is a book about how Bowie collected influences, ideas, musicians and other creatives. In his famous 1973 interview with Russell Harty, he explained:

> *I can take on the guises of different people that I meet. I can switch accents within seconds of meeting somebody and adopt their accent. I've always found that I collect. I'm a collector. I've always just seemed to collect personalities… ideas.*

Throughout his career, Bowie collected ideas, people, influences, opinions, and other stimuli. These he would combine and refabricate so that the original influences were unrecognisable and something entirely novel was fashioned. From Mick Ronson he collected musical arrangements. He collected the same from Tony Visconti, and also his production know-how. From Nile Rodgers, he gathered a hit machine. From Reeves Gabrels he collected wildly creative songwriting and guitar-led ideas. But it wasn't just people he was encountering – it was stimuli. In a 1976 *Playboy* interview, he was asked if he considered himself an original thinker, to which he replied, "Not by any means. More like a tasteful thief. The only art I'll ever study is stuff that I can steal from. I do think that my plagiarism is effective."

For Bowie, to absorb and reconstitute influences was not in any way negative. The maxim from Ecclesiastes: "What has been will be again; what has been done will be done again; there is nothing new under the sun" was never truer than with Bowie. How many artists can genuinely claim that their works are based on original thought? Perhaps Bowie is just more honest than others.

This book tells the stories of Bowie's career as revealed through interviews for the magazine. A career during which Bowie's profound sense of art and artifice was combined with a sponge-like ability to absorb the zeitgeist and deliver to the world something that was almost always entirely new, exciting and full of possibilities.

And so the story goes…

Chapter 1

AN OCCASIONAL DREAM

It was with the advent of the Spiders that Bowie found the formula he needed to carry the news to the masses. A solid band. If the previous years had been marked by Bowie moving from one band to the next searching for the right ingredients, the three years from 1971 to 1973 were notable for their relative stability – a period that began in 1969 with one John Cambridge, invariably known as Cambo. Kevin Cann, the noted Bowie authority, does not exaggerate when he says that "John Cambridge single-handedly altered the trajectory of popular music."

Growing up in Hull, the 12-year-old John began his music career as almost all drummers do – using knitting needles to tap along with the records of the day. As those days were the mid '60s, that meant the Shadows, the Dave Clark Five and Johnny Kidd & the Pirates. Some two years later, in what could be regarded as a *Sliding Doors* moment, he found himself at a club called the Kontiki when the band, a Driffield group called the Roadrunners, returned for their second set without their drummer. As they stood awkwardly on the stage waiting for the tardy stickman, a friend of John's shouted, "John will stand in while he comes back, won't you, John?" As John puts it, "My career as a drummer had begun." That *Sliding Doors* moment is just one of several surrounding John which, had fate taken a different route, could have meant a different career history for David Bowie.

The thriving Hull music scene of the time had also produced a capable guitarist by the name of Mick Wayne – a member of the Hullabaloos along with Cambo. Wayne would go on to play with David Bowie and famously played the solo on 'Space Oddity', setting in motion a series of events that would lead to the advent of the Spiders from Mars. The Hull scene was as fluid as it was lively at that time, with drummers and guitarists seemly swapping bands and standing in for one another as and when needed. So it was that Cambo, having turned down a previous offer, eventually agreed to join local band the Rats as their drummer. It was as a Rat that John struck up a friendship with Mick Ronson. Later, Woody Woodmansey was to replace John in the Rats, a move that also foreshadowed upcoming events with Bowie's future band, Hype/the Spiders from Mars.

The combo of Cambo and Ronno – clearly it was a thing to add an "o" suffix to form a nickname – proved a potent one and the Rats, already popular, came to be regarded as the top local band. Meanwhile, Mick Wayne's band, now called Junior's Eyes, were also making a name for themselves, gigging in London and getting airplay nationally. Later, in May 1969, Mick Wayne invited John to come and see his band Junior's Eyes and casually asked him to sit in on a song. Unbeknown to him, he was being auditioned and a few days later became a member of the band. So, it was off to London.

The road that led to Bowie was unfolding. David Bowie had a song called 'Space Oddity' and was set to record it with Tony Visconti. But though the producer assures me that he likes the song now, he regarded it at that time as a throwaway novelty song and declined to produce. Gus Dudgeon therefore did the honours for that track while Tony produced the remaining tracks on the subsequent album. The guitarist who played the iconic solo on the 'Space Oddity' track was one Mick Wayne and, when the time came to record the album, Tony said, "Why don't we get your band in?" – which seemed preferable to getting in, as John puts it, "this bass player and this drummer" for the various songs. Bowie and John met in July 1969 just days before starting to work together and hit it off immediately. The fabled proto-Spiders band, Hype, was formed.

Tony Visconti was the one to formally introduce Cambo and David. David stood out, even then. Whereas most of the band wore denim and long hair, David's hair was permed, and he habitually wore knitted jumpers and bright red or turquoise corduroy trousers. Bowie talked through the songs with John without playing them, which seems an unusual approach. To John, it seemed Bowie was intelligent and different with something interesting to say in any situation. Recording of David's new album commenced on 16 July. The album, like the one he had made two years earlier, would be called *David Bowie*, perhaps by way of a reset after the lack of success of the previous record. The tracks 'Janine', 'An Occasional Dream' and 'Letter to Hermione', David's plaintive message to his lost love, were recorded that day. It was David's practice to sit atop a high stool and play the songs on a 12-string guitar. There was no rehearsal before a take and usually the first or second take would be used: Bowie believed that early takes, even if they contained a few mistakes, always had a spontaneous quality that later ones lacked. The practice of preferring early takes continued throughout Bowie's career, as many musicians attest.

Over the following months, Cambo had many adventures with the band. In Cambo's book *Bowie, Cambo and All the Hype* he talks about a memorable occasion, the band left Dunfermline for Glasgow, leaving John behind in the toilet. John then caught a bus to the gig, arriving before the band, who, not having missed him, were surprised to find him awaiting their arrival. On another occasion, John and David walked into a music shop in Edinburgh and found the sheet music for 'Space Oddity'. On purchasing the item, Bowie studied it and remarked, "They've got the bloody chords wrong!"

It is a measure of Cambo and Bowie's close relationship that as early as February 1970, Cambo talks about David and Angie joining him on a trip to Hull, staying with his parents while Tony Visconti and his fiancée Liz Hartley stayed with other relatives of John's.

* * *

As many would-be musicians know, real-life and creeping grown-up responsibilities have scuppered the promising careers of many a young band. So, it was with guitarist Mick Wayne whose partner, Charlotte, was ill, forcing him to miss a few gigs. Junior's Eyes began to realise their chance had passed. John had continued with the band alongside his work with Bowie for a time, but by January 1970 it was clear that if things were going to happen for the band, they would have done by this point. The decision was made to end the band and in the absence of Wayne, Tim Renwick, guitarist from the *Space Oddity* album, deputised with Hype, but he had other work lined up and a more permanent solution was needed.

Quite why John Cambridge pursued the matter is still a mystery – even to John himself. What is clear is that he was pretty sure he had the solution to Bowie's guitar problem in Mick Ronson, his friend from the Rats. The problem was that Ronson had tried his hand as a guitarist in London before, and his efforts had earned him only an unreleased track by Elton John and a lot of debt. To persuade him to try his luck in the big city once more would be a challenge. Likewise, David Bowie and Tony Visconti were singularly unenthusiastic at the prospect of John's old mate from Hull becoming their new guitar player.

"No, he's really good. Look, I'm going home between gigs. Let me bring him back with me – see what you think," he implored. David and Tony casually waved him away. What did a drummer know about guitarists?

A classically trained pianist who also played violin and recorder, Ronson was also a talented arranger, but at this time he was working as a municipal gardener. John caught up with him as he marked out the lines of a school playing field with creosote. It must have been quite something to have seen an unenthusiastic Ronson walking away to mark the pitch, followed by John imploring him to give London another shot. The guitarist's reluctance was palpable and understandable given his previous experience and what was on offer – essentially a meeting with a one-hit wonder. "I'm not going down there again," said Ronson – monosyllabic at the best of times. "I've been ripped off too many times – not interested." Even as he appealed to Ronson to consider a meeting, John wondered to himself what he was doing walking around a playing field asking an unresponsive guitarist to meet an uninterested singer to form a partnership that seemed to appeal to neither of them.

John's final shot was, "Look, we're playing the Marquee Club next Tuesday and it's Junior's Eyes' last gig. Why don't you come along, bring your guitar and see what you think?" Ronson, at last, capitulated. But for John's persistence there would be no "Spider with the platinum hair."

It was an inauspicious start, the show wrongly billed as being Dave Berry, the 1960s' teen idol. John played his final gig with Junior's Eyes, followed by his first with Bowie's Hype. Ronson, who had been driven there in Cambridge's Hillman Minx, was introduced to David and the group then headed off to La Chasse, a nearby club, and from there to Haddon Hall – the sprawling Victorian villa where David and various musicians, artists and hangers-on, resided. Ronson picked up a guitar and David joined in. While others eventually drifted off to bed, Bowie and Ronson continued through the night and clearly hit it off – so much so that Bowie impulsively but enthusiastically asked Ronson to join him to play on John Peel's show in just two days' time. An equally enthused Ronson agreed, and a partnership was formed. There is no record of whether John was thanked.

David, in true self-effacing fashion, much later described the Peel session as going "very badly", but to many ears, it went rather well. The overall impression is one of a slightly shambolic but joyful romp. Reflecting on the occasion decades later, Ronson stated, "I didn't know any of the material. I was really nervous." Ronson positioned himself judiciously so that he could see what David was playing. "I just followed David – watched his fingers on the guitar. I guess it worked OK because he wanted to work with me again." Indeed, Bowie was sufficiently impressed that when asked by Peel on air if they were planning to do more gigs together, he asked Ronson, "Are we, Michael?" He wasn't sure if Ronson would be up for it, pointing out that he'd just come from Hull and they had met only two days ago. As Kevin Cann points out, though, Ronson's skills were already evident after just two days – 'The Width of a Circle' profiting particularly – and Bowie knew he would benefit greatly.

It seemed that the band, with Mick Ronson on guitar, Tony Visconti on bass and John Cambridge on drums, was beginning to solidify into the stable group that Bowie needed. However, things would shift further still before true stability was achieved. In spite of his friendship with David and his role in bringing Ronson aboard, plans were soon afoot to oust Cambo. As John told me in 2022, "I brought Mick Ronson down early February. By early April I'd gone!" This has been seen as an early example of a certain ruthless streak that Bowie had when it came to hiring and firing musicians. Many associates of David attest to an element of mercilessness – particularly in his early days. In later years things would change and, reluctant to let people down, he ended up with a surfeit of musicians who performed and recorded on a rotating basis. Two drummers – Sterling Campbell and Zachary Alford; four guitarists – Earl Slick, Gerry Leonard, David Torn and Mark Plati; and two bass players – Gail Ann Dorsey and Plati again. But the focus of a struggling artist is very different from that of a global superstar, and the young David needed to make sure everything was lean and perfectly aligned so that he could take his shot.

Ronson travelled back to Hull alongside John, sorting out his affairs and resigning from his job, and then returned to London and moved into Haddon Hall – the large residence where David rented an apartment and which formed a base for a rotating cast of musicians and associates of Bowie, still then including Cambo ("the first lodger to sleep in the creepy gallery," according to Tony Visconti). To call Haddon Hall a commune would be a misrepresentation – it was one flat in a large hall – but it had the easy-going artistic vibe and relaxed approach to old-fashioned values that characterised the artistic landscape of the time. London's Roundhouse was the venue of the first gig of the new line-up, not yet billed as Hype, and is an occasion which has gone down in the annals of popular music history as the first glam rock gig. Their look was inspired by an evening David and Angie had spent in the company of photographer Ray Stevenson, a fan of superheroes. Angie Bowie and Tony's girlfriend Liz Hartley had worked hard to make costumes for the band and each member now took on a corresponding persona. Foreshadowing later preoccupations, Bowie plays Spaceman (though some good sources have him as Rainbowman, it seems that the names were all applied retrospectively); Visconti is the superhero Hypeman; Ronson is Gangsterman; and Cambo, Cowboyman (not Pirateman, as one book has it). By comparison with the other bands on the bill that night – Caravan, the Groundhogs and Bachdenkel, bands later described by David as "denim-y" – the proto-Hype band must have seemed as if they were from another world. Until now, pop music had been regarded as the forte of artists who directly expressed their desires, feelings and dissatisfactions. Glam rock, with its pretentions towards artifice and theatre and pantomime, was a significant departure in which performers played parts, leading popular music away from self-expression and towards performance.

In later years, Bowie was to explain that he had originally seen himself as a songwriter whose compositions would be performed by others. He himself was "much too shy" to perform as himself. Accordingly, in spite of performing throughout his pre-fame period, he also sold songs to others. Notably Paul Nicholas, who recorded Bowie's novelty song 'Over the Wall We Go' and later Peter Noone, whose version of 'Oh! You Pretty Things' was, in 1971, his only solo hit. Immediately prior to his success, Bowie had teamed up, and effectively taken over, a band called Rungk and renamed it Arnold Corns. Formed at Dulwich College, the band was matched through Bowie with frontman and fashion designer Freddie Burretti to perform Bowie's compositions. Freddie, aka Rudi Valentino, had no singing voice and Bowie himself supplied most of the recorded vocals. Likewise, Bowie's musicians took over the roles within the band. Nevertheless, it was intended as a front and a vehicle for Bowie's songs to be performed and recorded without the need for ther "shy" Bowie to perform as himself.

At Bowie's own behest, however, the era of performing as oneself was now coming to an end. With its artfulness and enactment, the regalia and show of the Roundhouse marked the birth of glam rock. "We died a death," was Bowie's later assessment of the show. Others in attendance had misgivings too. Tim Renwick, Hype's stand-in guitarist said, "It didn't feel right." Likewise, Bowie's soon-to-be ex-manager Kenneth Pitt, to whom Bowie had been close, said, "There wasn't a nice feeling there. Something was wrong." Despite the misgivings of the audience, Bowie later said, "I knew it was right."

Yet personnel changes were still to be made before he regarded it as absolutely right. In the meantime, there was the small matter of David's wedding to Angie at which John Cambridge was to serve as a witness. The wedding took place on 20 March 1970 at Marylebone Registry Office and David's mother Peggy, who was not invited, turned up, having heard about it in the local newspaper. When it came time for the register to be signed, she stood up and took John's place, at which David could only give a helpless shrug in John's direction. Later, David, no doubt wishing to alleviate any ill feeling, commented, "John was the best man, weren't you, John?"

I'll take it, thought John. Indeed "best man" seemed like an appropriate role for John. By now, David and John had become close friends. "We mucked about with water pistols. David, just used to come back to my place. We'd go to the pub together, all that sort of thing. Mess about," John reports. There are many examples of their closeness, based on a shared humour. On one occasion, David – who was always called Dave by John – and Cambo were in a pub in Beckenham when John decided to put some music on the jukebox. Seeing that they had a copy of 'Space Oddity', John selected it to play three times. As the pub was quiet, it came on straight away. "Oh, they've got my song here!" David remarked, quite chuffed. As the song came on again, David said, "John, you've done this, haven't you?"

"Shut up, David, 'cos you bloody love it!" was the Cambo response. This jokey relationship continued when, years later, at Bowie's fiftieth birthday party, they played a game of John's invention called the Knobbing Game, whereby they would replace the word *love* in song lyrics with the word *knob*. Hence, 'All My Knobbing' by the Beatles,

'You've Lost that Knobbing Feeling' by the Righteous Brothers, and the Percy Sledge classic 'When a Man Knobs a Woman'.

Life was fun as young men making their way in the music business, having some success and looking forward to possible future triumphs but there were more difficult times, too. About three weeks into the recording of the album, David's father, Haywood Stenton Jones, known as John, suddenly died from pneumonia. The emotional climate in David's childhood home could be described as cold, with David's half-brother Terry often rowing with his mother while his father withdrew. Nevertheless, it seems David and John had a closeness and David was certainly deeply affected by the loss. Just weeks later, 'Space Oddity' scored him his first major success and to have been denied the chance to share this vindication with his father must have been painful. The authors Peter and Leni Gillman report that for a week after his father passed away, he received a silent phone call at 5.30 each day, which he interpreted as a call from John to make sure all was well.

In April 1969, prior to the move to Haddon Hall, David had moved into a flat in Foxgrove Road, Beckenham, as the tenant of his friend Mary Finnigan. With youthful idealism, he went about setting up what was rather grandly called the Beckenham Arts Lab, later known as Growth. The idea was to create music and "mixed media" – whatever combination of dance, mine and the visual arts would grow organically from the people arranged around the nucleus of David and Mary. The "happenings" took place at the Three Tuns pub on Beckenham High Street, although much later, Bowie would reflect that very little happened at these happenings and that he was disappointed by the apathy and passivity of many of those associated. Still, in the first rush of excitement and enthusiasm of those early days, David and Mary organised a free festival to take place at Croydon Road Recreation Ground in Beckenham. The line-up included the Strawbs, Keith Christmas who had played guitar on the *Space Oddity* album, Gasworks and a host of others. Stalls sold jewellery and Tibetan items and there were theatrical performances and a puppet show. Bowie's future wife, Mary Angela Barnett, barbecued on a grill over a wheelbarrow. The occasion was to be immortalised in the song 'Memory of a Free Festival' which appeared on the *David Bowie/Space Oddity* album: "It was ragged and naïve / It was Heaven". In fact, having lost his father on the fifth of the month and having buried him just five days prior to the event, David's mood was understandably somewhat different from what he portrayed in the song. And in fairness, Bowie describes the mood of the event in the song as not being his own mood, and moves from reflective yearning about the gathering and into the realms of drug-fuelled fantasy in describing the visitation of "tall Venusians" among the gathered throng, so the song can hardly be intended as an accurate portrayal. Though Bowie performed, he was otherwise sombre and withdrawn. That said, the band played a reggae version of 'Space Oddity' for a laugh, so there was room for levity. As to who played in Bowie's band, the point is contested. Many books say it was Junior's Eyes who backed him, but John, a meticulous record keeper, states in his book that they were in fact completing an eight-show residency at the Star Club. Tony Visconti, on the other hand, recalls that he "played bass and John Cambridge (of Junior's Eyes) played drums" at the event.

* * *

Bowie had moved on from many bands at this point, but John was, arguably, the first individual that Bowie had dismissed.

Tensions emerged three days after the wedding, when the band was booked into Trident Studios in London's Soho district to record 'Memory of a Free Festival' and 'The Supermen'. As John reports, he had played 'The Supermen' live at the Roundhouse with David and so knew the song, but when it came to recording there was a tense atmosphere. "When I went into the studio," he recalls, "they said, 'Hey, John, come on. Give us a minute. Give us a minute'. In other words, 'Piss off!' Then they said, 'We've come up with this bit in the middle. It's a bit complicated.' I couldn't get it," says Cambo.

Mick Ronson "encouraged" John by walking up to the drum booth where he was playing and saying: "Come on. It's fucking easy," which only added to the pressure. David broke the tension and suggested that he and John go for a drink, leaving Ronson and producer/bass player Tony Visconti to work on the track. History doesn't record what Tony and Ronson talked about, but John certainly wondered whether replacing him with Mick Woody Woodmansey, the Driffield drummer and fellow Rat, was on the agenda that day. Ronson had previously confided in David and Tony that he knew a "better drummer" who had replaced John in the Rats, while David and Tony had also been discussing replacing John already.

On 7 April, the day came. John, in true commune fashion, was painting the ceiling at Haddon Hall when a car drew up on the gravel drive and he heard Angie saying: "Go on. You've got to tell him," while David protested: "John's a mate!" David asked him to come down from the ladder and then explained that he and the others had been thinking about getting in another drummer. Stressing that "It isn't you, John", he invited him to stay as long as he liked.

No doubt realising that things would be awkward if he stayed when Bowie was using a new drummer, John elected to leave the next morning and borrowed five pounds from David for the trip. This he spent on two Premium Bonds, which have allowed him to confirm for biographers that the date he left the band was 7 April. Later, John saw a contract signed by Hype, including Woody's name, dated four days earlier. It appears David had been building up to breaking the bad news for a while.

Asked last year, when I interviewed him, whether he regretted that his dream of stardom ended at the tender age of 20, John points out that Mick Ronson had three children and didn't live to see them grow up. When he joined the band, Ronson was a teetotal Mormon. John, on the other hand, liked a pint and therefore fears that, if the roles were reversed, he might well have not survived life on the road. "Mick would change places with me now, if he could," John says rightly. Mick Ronson scaled the heights as Bowie's wingman in the Spiders From Mars but died of bowel cancer at the too early age of 46 in 1993. "If I'd been there, I would have gone before Mick. Wouldn't have had kids or anything."

Cambo and Bowie remained friends and stayed in touch over the years, and John even attended Bowie's 50th birthday party in New York in 1997. The fact remains that without John insisting Mick Ronson come to London and join the band, there would be no Spiders from Mars. No Woody Woodmansey or Trevor Bolder playing with Bowie. The Spiders were the stable band that Bowie needed to launch his proper bid for fame – and it began the day John Cambridge met Bowie.

Chapter 2
STAR

There was much talk of Mick Ronson in 2022, when I had the very good fortune of interviewing Joe Elliott, lead singer of Def Leppard – the band whose album *Hysteria* outsold *Sgt. Pepper* in America. And I have always loved them – which is unusual for a Bowie fan. As Joe himself said in our interview, fans of Bowie are far more likely to be to also be fans of the Cure or Depeche Mode. There can't be many of us in the middle of the Bowie/Def Leppard Venn diagram, if indeed there even is such a thing. But I've always been a rock fan as well as a Bowie fan, but my weakness for layered harmonies and melodies, along with killer riffs and high production values, meant that Def Leppard had me hooked.

I knew Joe was a Bowie fan, of course. More than a fan. I'd seen him play an acoustic version of 'Ziggy Stardust' on one of the Def Leppard VHS videos I had when I was young. I'd heard Cybernauts, the band that Joe and Leppard colleague Phil Collen had formed with Woody Woodmansey and Trevor Bolder from the Spiders from Mars. I knew that he'd worked on the final album by Mick Ronson – the guitarist who will be the focus of this chapter eventually – and that he'd played at the memorial concert for Ronson, and I knew that Mike Garson played on Def Leppard's latest album.

When a group of Bowie alumni and stars played a series of tribute gigs in major cities, Joe was invited to sing at the London event and, to the slight bemusement of the Cure and Depeche Mode fans around me, I went a bit mad when he walked on stage to sing 'All the Young Dudes' and 'Suffragette City'.

I will be forever happy that I became so involved in Bowie fandom for so many reasons, but a big one is that it means I got to spend nearly two hours talking about Bowie with Joe Elliott. Of the many illuminating things that he said was that for the longest time, he regarded Bowie and the Spiders as a band. As a unit. Rather than thinking of Bowie as a solo artist, he thought of them as a band of brothers, just like other current bands like Mott the Hoople and T. Rex. Sure, those bands focused on the singer as almost all bands do, and the personnel changed at times, but fans regarded them as a unit. To many, it was a surprise when the Spiders fell by the wayside – well, were dismissed onstage at the Hammersmith Odeon – and Bowie made *Diamond Dogs* without them.

I think it was my good friend Nicholas Pegg who said that after Mick Ronson, Bowie never shared the stage with anyone else in the same way again. To the world, they appeared to be close partners – and were. Many people's first memory of Bowie is seeing him perform 'Starman' on *Top of the Pops* in 1972, and it will not have been lost on the audience that Ronson is almost as front and centre as Bowie – singing into the same mic as Bowie drapes his jumpsuited arm around Ronson's shoulder in what was seen by many as somewhat homoerotic but to me seems like a casual and relaxed mateyness. They were as much of a double act as they could possibly be.

A classic baby boomer, Michael Ronson was born in Hull on 26 May 1946, and was joined eleven years later by sister Maggi and five years later again by brother David. Born into a city recovering from a hard war, young Ronson, like most of his generation, was conditioned to seek the security of steady work and a trade that could bring the security that the war generation had lacked and therefore craved. Young Mick Ronson, however, began to show an aptitude for music when he picked up the family accordion. While his father George was the disciplinarian of the family, mum Minnie nurtured his talent and bought a piano and arranged lesson with a local teacher, Mrs Bolder, who was the grandmother of Trevor, the future bass player for the Spiders from Mars. Ronson became an accomplished player, also taking up and making excellent progress on the violin – although at times he avoided making a big deal of his talents, not only because he was naturally self-effacing but also to dodge adverse reactions from the streetwise kids of Hull. At times he even resorted to paying others to carry his violin case.

Despite his clear gift for the violin, the young Mick, inspired by Duane Eddy, the Rolling Stones and the Yardbirds, would wait until his teacher wasn't looking and then hold the violin like a guitar and pluck it in emulation of his heroes. It was clear that his future laying in the six-stringed plucked and strummed instrument, not the four-stringed bow. His first guitar was a Rosetti acoustic which cost £14. For a player of numerous instruments and with excellent music knowledge, he became a very good player in a short time, playing in local bands the Mariners and then the Crestas and building a solid reputation.

It is understandable that Ronson was reluctant when John Cambridge tried to persuade him, much later in January 1970, to go to London to try his luck with David Bowie. Ronson had tried that trip before, a few years earlier, working as a mechanic and playing with a band called the Voice. Although things looked hopeful for a while, with Mickie Most managing and an appearance on *Ready, Steady, Go!* promised, things took a bad turn when most of the band moved to the Bahamas, leaving Mick Ronson's equipment and that of drummer Dave Bradfield, in a bedroom for them to collect. After playing unsuccessfully with another band, the Wanted, Ronson wrote home saying, "Things are bad." After lethargy from the group and complaints from his flatmates about his guitar practice, Ronson finally wrote to say he was returning to Hull, settling into local band the Rats and taking steady work as a municipal gardener.

* * *

Prior to this, David had been working closely with British mime artist Lindsay Kemp. Kemp had used Bowie's 'When I Live My Dream' as opening music for his show *Clown's Hour* and Bowie went backstage to make himself known. Kemp later recalled that, "He fell in love with my world, you know, with my kind of circus world.... Afterwards he came backstage and expressed a desire to learn from me, to study with me. And it was love at first sight. I mean, the moment I saw him, God, love at first sight." Kemp was an important influence and a person from whom Bowie collected ideas and influences before reshaping and reusing them to create highly original popular art. Bowie became a student of Kemp's and learned the arts of mime and dance directly from him. Together, they created a show, *Pierrot in Turquoise* – turquoise being associated in Buddhism with everlastingness. Kemp recalled that he was responsible for keeping David interested in music and performance. He told the Canadian Broadcasting Corporation:

> *Just before I met David, he was planning on giving up music altogether. I mean, he was feeling very disillusioned. God he [worked] very hard and his manager … worked very hard to get him gigs but he felt he wasn't really going anywhere. When we met, he was in fact working in an office, you see. And had been studying Buddhism for quite a while, and in fact was planning on chucking the whole thing in, I mean music and so on. And going up to Scotland to a monastery to join a brotherhood of Tibetan monks. Well, I saved him from that [laughs].*

Bowie became enamoured with Kemp's world of performance and with Kemp himself, with whom he had a brief relationship. Until now, Bowie had adopted a range of images, but each was a plausible version of himself: mod; hippy; beatnik. He was not so much playing with characters as searching for an identity. It was through Lindsay Kemp that Bowie came to understand how to inhabit and represent a character other than his own. Kemp remembers:

> *Firstly, I told him that I wanted to see his spirit dancing. I really believe that movement is the soul's desire to be free. And therefore had to begin by kind of freeing him from his timidity, his shyness. I mean he was very keen, he had the desire, God knows, but it took a lot of gymnastics, physical*

> *work, to make his body more flexible. He certainly had the imagination of the dancer. But I told him, I encouraged him to be more audacious, you know, more experimental. To take risks and so on.*

Bowie took all of this and, in his first real act of collecting and reusing, started to work on characters for himself and his band. Mick Ronson arrived at exactly the right time to play his part. It was little over a month after Ronson's arrival that the band – Bowie, Visconti, Ronson and Cambo – found themselves on stage in costume playing characters rather than performing as themselves. While this might not seem particularly groundbreaking looking back from the twenty-first century, it was in fact a great departure from the approach to popular music to that point. Throughout the '50s and '60s, virtually all artists were regarded as speaking from the heart. Think of Dylan, for example, and we think of an artist who articulated his views and was the voice of a generation. Alone among their contemporaries, the Beatles had embraced layers of artifice and pretence with *Sgt. Pepper's Lonely Hearts Club Band* in which they played characters other than themselves. If we consider others – the Who, the Rolling Stones, the Kinks, James Brown, Simon & Garfunkel, Fleetwood Mac and any number of others – the common factor is that all are regarded as articulating their own thoughts and messages, or perhaps those of their contemporaries. Bowie and Ronson – and Tony and John – changed direction completely. They were not themselves on stage, they were characters. Their words and messages could no longer be taken as their own but from some other narrator. Unlike others, they were not spilling their heart's blood on the page (or stage). There was now a layer of artifice, performance and portrayal. This is the essence of what became glam rock or art rock. Rock music would be forever changed – if it caught on!

We now know that it did, but that was by no means certain at the time. Bowie had had his novelty hit with 'Space Oddity' the year before, but a successful follow-up was not forthcoming. There were to be many machinations and adjustments before the final successful formula was devised. First, as already described, the services of John Cambridge were brutally dispensed with – at the instigation of Ronson. "Little by little, Ronno replaced the group with other mates from Hull," Tony Visconti commented years later.

This act of cold-bloodedness was perhaps essential for eventual success, and Mick Ronson had form. In a strange series of events, Ronson had dismissed Cambo from the Rats in April 1969 and replaced him with Mick "Woody" Woodmansey – an act that in turn led to Cambo joining Junior's Eyes, which became Bowie's backing band, and then to Cambo recruiting Ronson. Given Ronson's track record, it perhaps should be no surprise that the same happened with Hype. But when it came to getting the personnel he wanted, this was David's first go at being ruthless. The elements of the Spiders from Mars were forming at the behest of Ronson, and Bowie was learning a ruthlessness that he would use later when tough decisions about personnel needed to be made.

Shifting loyalties were a feature of this time. Hadn't Ronson and Woody ditched David in August 1970 and returned to Hull, leaving Bowie to play a gig solo? The eventual onstage sacking of Woody and bassist Trevor Bolder at the Hammersmith Odeon in 1973 is perhaps more understandable in view of the history. For now, though, the band settled into working on a new album, which was to become *The Man Who Sold the World*. Mick Ronson was to play a vital role in its creation. The debt to the Beatles' concept was confirmed by Tony Visconti, who says that the album was intended to be their *Sgt. Pepper*.

Whereas much of Bowie's career is – among many other things – marked by the collection and repurposing of ideas to wildly creative effect, for *The Man Who Sold the World*, he relied on the ideas of others for a completely different reason – apathy! The newly married David was, as Tony recalls, "holding hands with Angie and going 'coochie-coochie-coo'," so Mick Ronson and Tony Visconti stepped up. Notions that David had little creative input seem a little wide of the mark – Bowie certainly wrote the songs – but it is true to say that the band had a large amount of unsupervised freedom to make their own arrangements and create – and create they did.

Given that Ronson had such a degree of freedom in the studio and that heroes were Cream and Jeff Beck, it is unsurprising that the resultant album is characterised by Ronson's stamp of British rock-style arrangements and prominent distorted guitars. The glam rock artifice is in evidence too. The personal confessional lyrics of the previous album, *Space Oddity* (originally known, in common with his 1967 album, as *David Bowie*), have not been completely eliminated, but they are less in evidence and instead, character-driven pieces are in evidence, such as in 'Saviour Machine', and 'The Supermen'.

By the time recording had ended, Tony Visconti had had enough of trying to drag David out of bed for a vocal or to finish a lyric and was far from enamoured with the pushy style of David's new manager, Tony Defries. Tony had also been producing T. Rex and Marc Bolan, who was desperate to record day and night, so Tony told a bewildered and surprised David that he was going to concentrate his efforts elsewhere.

By the summer of 1971, the album had sold a mere 1395 copies in the United States and even fewer in the UK. Bowie's producer and bass player had left in favour of Bolan, and his drummer and guitarist had returned to their hometown to seek their fortune there. Needless to say, there was little at this time to suggest that within a few short years, Bowie would go on to achieve great international acclaim first with Woody and Ronson and a little later with Tony.

Mick Ronson returned to live with his parents while Woody moved in with his girlfriend and future wife, June. Ronson put together a group consisting of himself, Woody, Tony and Rats singer Benny Marshall on vocals, initially calling it Hype before eventually settling on Ronno. "We've left Bowie. Do you want to do the vocal?" Woody asked Benny on the latter's doorstep. "Yeah, I wouldn't mind," said Marshall, and the deal was done. The band had a recording contract with Philips and could live in Hull far more cheaply than they could in London. Tony, although a member of the band, remained largely in London working with Bolan, so Ronson brought in local boy Trevor Bolder as a sub and it was this line-up, the Spiders in all but name, that recorded a single. With no songwriter in the band, though, a planned album stalled.

Both Bowie and Ronson were at a low ebb, but as a result they were both ready to try something different. In May '71, David called and, as Ronson related in 1986, asked, "Aren't you fed up with being back in Hull?" Ronson was. "Just catch the first train," David advised. Ronson did so and the path to stardom, previously interrupted, was restored for both.

The trio of Ronson, Woody and Trevor moved into Haddon Hall and began rehearsing Bowie's material – also finding time to record tracks for Dana Gillespie and play a Radio 1 session. At last, Bowie had a more settled band. One that had experience of solid gigging in Hull away from the limelight and was both tight and solid. Gone was the ramshackle cast of musicians and the power trio of Ronson, Bolder and Woody Woodmansey proved to be leagues ahead of the shambling *Space Oddity* guitar jams. It cannot be entirely coincidental that, as an artist who had been releasing records with an ever-changing cast of characters since 1964, it was only when the Spiders had spun their web around Bowie's songs that he found success.

Recording contracts were murderous in those days, usually requiring at least an album a year, so it was time to record another, this time for RCA – *Hunky Dory*. Interestingly, *Hunky Dory* co-producer Ken Scott later said that he believed Bowie had started to feel that Tony's influence on his music was too strong. He had come to be bassist, producer and string arranger, and Bowie was beginning to fear that his own contribution to his own music was being swamped. Quite how this fits with the idea that it was Tony who was fed up with Bowie's lack of enthusiasm is perhaps difficult to fathom, but the two perspectives are not mutually exclusive. And, with the departure of Tony, Bowie did have an excellent replacement; for arrangements and strings he could now rely on Mick Ronson. It is perhaps telling that, three years later, when the partnership broke up, it was Tony who again took up writing the arrangements.

For now, though, the way was clear for Mick Ronson to really make his presence felt on the new album. Trevor had taken up the mantle on bass, but it was Ronson who filled the void as band leader and string arranger. Not that he had a history of writing arrangements for strings, but he did read music, so David had casually told Dana Gillespie: "It's all right. Mick does string arrangements," and Ronson had risen to the occasion. It's curious to reflect on how different songs like 'Life on Mars?' could have been without Mick's strings or with strings by another arranger. In his notes to the 2008 *iSelectBowie* compilation, the man himself says that "Mick Ronson created one of his first and best string parts" for the song.

Authors Rupert Creed and Garry Burnett report in their excellent book *The Mick Ronson Story* that Ronson was daunted by this, having never performed the role before, but he grasped the nettle and used the piano at the family home in Hull to write the arrangements while Bowie in more southerly climes worked on the songwriting. While Ronson's strings on 'Life on Mars?' are rightly celebrated, his arrangements on 'Fill Your Heart' and 'Quicksand' are equally sumptuous and set the tone for the album. Producer Ken Scott, who engineered for the Beatles among others, has said that Ronson's natural ability is what made him special as an arranger: "he didn't really know what he was supposed to do so he was much freer." While *Hunky Dory* is often thought of as a folk-influenced album, it is raised beyond the status of a genre piece by two things – Ronson's strings and Ronson's guitar. The guitar interplay on 'Andy Warhol' juxtaposes resonant open chords with a walking, skipping hook, and elevates the track from folk strum to a sophisticated back and forth – albeit with a riff that, as

Nicholas Pegg points out, is lifted from Ron Davies's 'Silent Song Through the Land' – a typical example of Bowie's collection and repurposing. Elsewhere on the album, 'Changes' make reference to the layers of artifice and theatre now permeating his work: "So I turned myself to face me / But I've never caught a glimpse / Of how the others must see the faker / I'm much too fast to take that test." He thus establishes himself as pop's greatest dismantler and assembler.

It had been mooted that the Velvet Underground's 'White Light/White Heat', a track from their eponymous 1968 album, would be recorded for inclusion. In the event, it was replaced by Bowie's own homage to the band, 'Queen Bitch', Bowie's handwritten sleeve notes on the reverse of the album making this clear ('some V.U. White Light returned with thanks'). 'White Light/White Heat', Lou Reed's treatise on speed and astral projection, became a live staple for Bowie for decades to come and he even duetted on the song alongside Reed at Bowie's 50th birthday concert. Indeed, the entire second side of the album can be seen as an act of collecting because it brings together not only Bowie's tribute to Reed and his band but also 'Andy Warhol', 'Song for Bob Dylan', and the Biff Rose cover 'Fill Your Heart'.

However, to return to Ronson's role, the sound of his thin distorted Les Paul played through a half open wah-wah and fed into a Marshall amp – a sound so evident on 'Queen Bitch' – is at least as influential as his string arrangements in lifting the album from folky nothingness to a varied but cohesive proto-glam art rock piece. *Hunky Dory* consistently ranks as first or second in music press lists of the best Bowie albums (often alternating with *Low*). In their excellent biography of Mick Ronson, Weird and Gilly quote Joe

Elliott, Steve New and Chrissie Hynde all crediting Ronson as the musician who elevated the album. In conversation with me, Joe also said:

> *Look at 'Queen Bitch'! In another universe, I would have befriended David Bowie and said, "'I've got an idea. Let's put 'It Ain't Easy' on Hunky Dory and let's put 'Queen Bitch' on Ziggy Stardust.' And then you've got your Sgt. Pepper right there. So, for me, Ziggy's always going to get 9½ stars. I've talked to Trevor Bolder and Woody. They were recorded like five days apart. Bowie still had his Hunky Dory hair when he recorded Ziggy Stardust. It's only the way it was presented to us after the fact that we think it's a different time period. So, they made a lot of choices. I went, "Why did you leave 'Velvet Goldmine' off Ziggy Stardust? Why would you leave 'Holy Holy' off?"*

Those five days are a testament to the punishing schedule but also to the wild creativity of Bowie and Ronson. *Hunky Dory* had been released on RCA, thanks to a deal brokered by Bowie's manager Tony Defries and the next album, which would be named *The Rise and Fall of Ziggy Stardust and the Spiders from Mars* would be the one to break Bowie as a major artist. Recording of that album started before *Hunky Dory* had even been released. Incredibly, it was to be his fifth album. It was also to be the album on which Bowie's collectorship, and his ability to adopt and inhabit a character reached its zenith – with perilous results, and always with Mick Ronson by his side.

After Tony left and the band broke up, Bowie hadn't toured with *Hunky Dory*, but now he set about creating a character to inhabit on stage rather than take the stage as himself. In a 1983 interview quoted in Vox magazine, he explained:

> *As an adolescent, I was painfully shy, withdrawn. I didn't really have the nerve to sing my songs on stage, and nobody else was doing them. I decided to do them in disguise so that I didn't have to actually go through the humiliation of going on stage and being myself.*

So it was that, in his supreme act of collection, he began to assemble a character to perform his songs. Using Freddie Burretti to play the character for him hadn't yielded success – it's interesting to speculate about how Bowie's career might have progressed if Arnold Corns had found the fame that he had intended for them – so he himself must play the character. David might be too shy to dress and perform outrageously on stage, but Ziggy wasn't. Chris O'Leary reports on a famous incident when Bowie, on his first trip to America, spoke at length to the Velvet Underground's Doug Yule while all the time believing him to be Lou Reed. (To be fair, there was some physical resemblance.) He later realised or was informed of his error and felt that the notion of meeting a faux individual and yet having all the same feelings, reactions and enjoyment as would have come from meeting the "genuine" article, was intriguing and full of possibilities. Wouldn't an audience respond to the fakery and artifice of a pop music performer in the same way he unwittingly had? And with all the sensations and wonder that they would have with a performer who was attempting to portray themselves in some kind of authentic way? What was authenticity anyway? Barthes' theory of the death of the author, which holds that meaning originates in the audience not the author, had separated the author from authenticity – and Bowie could simply take the idea to its logical conclusion, in the same way that Andy Warhol, a man he had recently met, had sent actor Allen Midgette to appear as him on a 1967 university lecture tour.

Bowie had the skills to create and portray a character from his time with Lindsay Kemp, as well as his own natural ability. Inspired, Bowie began to assemble a ready-made rock star from spare parts he found. The Ziggy character was never fully drawn nor the backstory fleshed out and Bowie gave a few conflicting accounts of Ziggy's story as things progressed. The story, such as it was, was written only after the album was completed. The overall narrative is of a rock star, possibly an alien, bringing his message to a world on the brink of annihilation, but the narrative isn't the point, it's the postmodern fragmentary nature of the collected and reassembled images that characterise the piece. Mr Stardust himself was generally believed to be either an alien or a prophet or both – this Bowie took from Vince Taylor, the English rock 'n' roller, who had suffered with mental health problems and believed himself to be God or an alien. Certain moves Bowie took from Gene Vincent, who was injured in a car accident and performed wearing a splint. Said Bowie, "It meant that to crouch at the mike, as was his habit, he had to shove his injured leg out behind him to, what I thought, great theatrical effect. This rock stance became position number one for the embryonic Ziggy."

The Ziggy name came as a variation of Iggy [Pop] and from the name of a tailor's shop, whereas 'Stardust' was lifted from the name of the psychobilly singer known as the Legendary Stardust Cowboy. Costume is so often at the heart of inhabiting any character, and Bowie initially turned to his friend Freddie Burretti for his famous suit inspired by a circuit board which he wore tucked into knee-high boots in a look lifted from *A Clockwork Orange*, as Mark Paytress notes in the most comprehensive publication on the subject, *Bowiestyle*. Suzi Fussey, his mum's hairdresser who would later accompany him on tour and marry Mick Ronson, cut his hair into the short backed, long fringed early Ziggy cut. As Paytress says, "Prior to Glam Rock, rock musicians found the issue of stardom faintly embarrassing. Bowie, by building the concept into Ziggy Stardust, was able to join the new breed of 'Superstars' while simultaneously managing to transcend stardom's most sordid associations by merely 'playing' at the role." The effect was at once electrifying and destabilising. What were we to make of this superstar being – for that was what he was to become? Could we believe anything of what we saw? Could we equate the alien street urchin Ziggy on the stage with the artist/actor David Bowie who portrayed him? Throughout the history of popular music, the person on the stage was regarded largely as the narrator of their songs. Whose voice was this? David's? Or the voice of Ziggy as written by David? And who was David Bowie anyway? Another character, perhaps, somewhat removed from David Jones? As Bowie said: "it's all artifice", and the layers of artifice were intriguing and exhilarating to audiences accustomed to sincere scruffy denim-clad men singing their manifestos.

"I pieced together bits and pieces of other artists, and they all became this rather grand, stylish lad, Ziggy," he said reflectively in a Radio 1 broadcast on his 50th birthday. Earlier, as quoted in the Bowie chapter of the book *Valentines & Vitriol* (1977), he put it more neatly: "I'm an instant star. Just add water and stir."

Two images cemented Bowie and Ronson as a partnership in the minds of the public. Ask any fan of the right generation when they first became aware of Bowie and, like Joe Elliott who kicked off this chapter, they'll probably tell you that it was that breakthrough performance of 'Starman' on *Top of the Pops* that had the impact. It was this performance that the kids were talking about in British schools the morning after and it was the particular moment when Bowie points at the camera, swivels his hand and sings, "so I picked on you – oo – oo" that is remembered as the instant when he individually picked out hundreds of thousands of young people to be his followers. But there was another moment – just as striking. The sharing of the mic in that *TOTP* performance. Clearly, this was not a solo act but a partnership. Anyone who had seen the Mick Rock photo of Bowie simulating fellatio on Ronson's guitar would have been in little doubt anyway. It's impossible to imagine coy David doing such a thing, but wild boy Ziggy inhabited a different universe.

"This is going to be something new … no one has ever seen anything like this before … it's going to be entertainment. That's what's missing in pop music now," said Bowie in June 1972.

The recording of *Ziggy Stardust* commenced at Trident studios in November 1971 – not only a month before the release of *Hunky Dory* but around 6 weeks after Bowie and the as yet unnamed Spiders played their first gig at Friars Aylesbury. By the time recording started, the band was tight and well-rehearsed. The presence of Ronson is felt strongly throughout *Ziggy Stardust.* The album famously launches with Woody Woodmansey's drums, played with metronomic timing without cymbals or flourishes, signalling the end of the world and setting the scene for the LP. As Woody told me, who cares about cymbals when the planet is doomed?

The Bowie that Ronson encountered in the studio was very different from the one he had worked with two albums ago on *The Man Who Sold the World*. Gone was the guy who had to be cajoled out of bed to do a vocal or write a lyric. No more canoodling with Angie. This Bowie was highly focused. Far from leaving Ronson and the rest to work out the music themselves, Bowie wanted this album to match his vision precisely – even to the extent of humming solos to Ronson so that he could match them on guitar. "Every single note and every part of the song had to be exactly as I heard it in my head," he recalled – and this happened "at least in my mind". "An awful lot of that was just me telling him what notes I wanted," he continued. Ronson, for his part, was characteristically laid-back and happy to oblige. All of which perhaps serves perhaps to underplay Ronson's wild creativity on this album. Unleashed from the shackles of its previous Arnold Corns arrangement, 'Moonage Daydream', the standout Ronson track, sweeps and soars. The album opener had started with Woody's drums – as had the second track, 'Soul Love'.

A pattern had been established and an expectation set – only so that it could be torn down and ripped to shreds. Staking his claim early, Ronson startles as he launches into repeated staccato power chord intro before the track quickly relaxes into a 12-string strum, accompanied by an urgent vocal from Bowie which always seems on the verge of breaking out and losing control. Ronson reminds us of his presence at the end of each verse as if barely able to contain himself for what is to come, while Bowie/Ziggy asserts his shifting identities. As author Peter Doggett further points out, Bowie declares himself tough and resilient – an alligator; a mama/papa (gender ambiguous); and the space invader that we know Ziggy to be. Peter Doggett is right on the money when he says that the track would have been quickly and rightly forgotten if the weak Arnold Corns rendering had been the only recorded version. It is the guitar of Ronson – along with vastly improved lyrics and production from Ken Scott – which elevates the track.

The history and development of the track, from the feeble Arnold Corns recording to the pile-driving *Ziggy Stardust* version, demonstrates the essential partnership between David Bowie and Mick Ronson. Bowie has the vision, the ideas and the visualisation. Ronson has the tools, the talent and the graft to realise it. Simon Goddard puts it beautifully:

> *David's is the architect's brain but Mick's is the engineer's. David hears overall shapes; Mick hears supporting structures. With every day he spends in a studio, Mick's harmonic instincts finesse. He arranges music in such a way that it doesn't sound like something added but something revealed, like a secret layer that had always been there, like old wallpaper just waiting for his roll-up-tightening fingers to peel back and expose.*

Although Goddard is talking mainly about Ronson and Bowie's production partnership on Lou Reed's *Transformer* here, the relationship is never more in evidence than in the contrast between these two versions of 'Moonage Daydream'. It was a heady mixture perfect for the early '70s zeitgeist and set against a grim backdrop of strikes, uncollected rubbish littering streets and power cuts in contemporary Britain. Stardust couldn't help but shine. Trevor Bolder, from the eye of the storm, felt the winds of change:

> *I suppose we were recording Hunky Dory and Ziggy Stardust at the same time, as David already knew what direction he wanted to go in. As soon as we recorded 'Moonage Daydream' I knew something was going to happen. After listening to the guitar solo, I just thought, This is going to be amazing, this is going to go somewhere. This is special. And then it did, you know. That was the point when I knew, Hang on, there's something special here. This is going to be really, really good.*

Bowie felt it too, "I'm going to be huge and it's quite frightening in a way, because I know that when I reach my peak and it's time for me to be brought down, it will be with a bump."

That bump, if it ever came, was a very long way off. The 'Starman' *TOTP* moment was the 1972 equivalent of going viral in the minds of Britain's youth. The tour, which started in the Toby Jug pub in Tolworth in February, grew and grew, visiting the US twice, becoming the Aladdin Sane tour, taking on new costumes and identities, notably Japanese kabuki-style robes designed by Kansai Yamamoto, and culminating in the final concert at the Hammersmith Odeon on 3 July 1973. In the meantime, *Aladdin Sane* had been recorded, with Ronson as influential as ever, and also sharing the limelight with new pianist Mike Garson, who added the sublimely trashy piano to tracks such as 'Lady Grinning Soul' and the title track. 'The Jean Genie' became Bowie's first top three single and featured Ronson's

Bo Diddley/John Lee Hooker riff prominently. On 'Star' on the *Ziggy* album, Bowie had anticipated the joys of stardom to come: "So inviting, so enticing to play the part," and dreaming wistfully that he, "could fall asleep at night" and "fall in love all right / As a rock and roll star."

Of course, he took it all too far… stardom comes quickly, and Bowie was right to be scared. Soon, he played the part full-time, conflating David Jones/Bowie with the Ziggy Stardust role. In interviews he adopted a mannered voice and included erudite-sounding superfluous words to add to the mystic and alienness. Simultaneously, his manager, Tony Defries, who was bankrolling Bowie in exchange for half of everything – after Bowie alone had paid the expenses – decided that it would be a good idea to insist that David act like the star he was to become and that everyone else should treat him thus. Therefore, Defries forbade Bowie to open doors for himself and denied interviews requested by important publications – long before Bowie had in fact achieved any notable success but fully in keeping with the artifice and mystique with which he had enveloped himself. For a still young Bowie, used to experimenting with his identity but unused to inventing and inhabiting one, it was too much to hope that he would keep his feet on the ground at a time when his head was in the stars. "I became Ziggy Stardust," he said in 1976. "David Bowie went totally out the window. Everybody was convincing me that I was a messiah ... I got hopelessly lost in the fantasy." As Woody Woodmansey puts it, Ziggy Stardust was more powerful than David Bowie. Relations between the band and Bowie deteriorated as the musicians became well known in their own rights. Bowie, it seems, hadn't expected his backing band to come to be regarded as part of the package.

The fantasy would have to end. Finally, it was only partly Bowie's doing. Pianist Mike Garson, who had contributed such arresting piano on *Aladdin Sane*, joined the band on tour. Known as Garson the Parson, he enjoyed conversation with the rest of the band and entourage – mainly on the subject of the Church of Scientology, of which he was a committed member. One day, Woody Woodmansey sat next to Mike. Looking at a piece about Lamborghinis in a magazine, he commented on their loveliness. "You can buy one after the tour," said Mike.

"Yeah, I wish!" replied Woody, reeling at the thought of purchasing a car with a price tag of around $20,000. "How much do you think I earn?" he asked a surprised-looking Garson. It transpired that Mike was pulling in ten times what Woody was being paid (some sources say four times but either way …). "But you've been with Bowie since the beginning!" Mike remarked, not unreasonably.

This was all the more surprising because, as Woody says in his autobiography, Bowie had previously called the Spiders out for the evening and carefully explained to them, "I really want to prepare you for what's coming. You're going to be millionaires and I want to prepare you for that." He was absolutely serious.

Further investigations revealed that other musicians on the tour were also being paid more than Trevor and Woody. Sharing his findings with his fellow Spiders, he found both men similarly outraged. Ronson, who knew Lou Reed's manager, said he would arrange a deal with him, and the band was quickly offered $100,000 for first refusal on a record deal for the Spiders from Mars.

Inevitably, Bowie and manager Tony Defries, got wind of things and a meeting was hastily arranged. A hard-nosed impresario, Defries, infamously, had taken control of Bowie's career and ploughed huge sums that he didn't have into creating a star. It was all artifice, of course, but that was all that was needed. This period in Bowie's story deserves a book of its own. We don't have space for an in-depth exploration here, but it's well worth a substantial detour. There could be no better exemplification of the supreme act of theatre, bluff and artful pretence that made Bowie a superstar.

* * *

When Defries took over Bowie's affairs, it was an act of faith. Bowie had been trying for years and, notwithstanding his number five hit with 'Space Oddity', he hadn't made any inroads. And the fact that the success of that single was tied to what was at that time being referred to as the "moonshot" meant that it was easy for people to construct a narrative around the notion that Bowie was a one-hit wonder. Bowie's previous manager, Ken Pitt, adored David and had handled his affairs with dedication but with limited means and vision. After Bowie wrote to tell him he no longer considered him to be his manager, Olav Wyper, Philips Records' general manager, had given him the number of his lawyer, Tony Defries, to help sort out the legal niceties of the extrication. With natural English reserve and a large degree of guilt, he was reticent about taking the next step, but Angie was the kind of wife whose American straightforwardness pushed David on. "You *must* see the man Olav told you about," she implored, urging David to take what she regarded as a painful but necessary step just as she had with the dismissal of John Cambridge. Many people I have spoken to endorse the notion that Bowie may not have made it without Angie – or indeed, without Tony Defries.

When David entered the office, he was immediately aware that he had walked onto a stage and that Defries was playing the central role. Defries stared at David, making him even more nervous than he had been – which was quite a lot. The lawyer, for his part, regarded David, in common with most of his clients, as simply someone whose affairs he needed to sort out. As Tony Zanetta, later Bowie's tour manager and a senior figure in his company, MainMan, puts it:

> *Defries led David to his office and ushered him into a seat. He calmly took his place behind his desk, slowly picked up his phone, and ordered tea. Then he seemed to fall into deep thought. He picked up the phone again and in a soft, soothing voice began to discuss another matter with his secretary. Defries turned to the papers on his desk, thumbing through and rearranging them. He made another call. Then tea arrived.*

He was playing a role.

Defries explained that David's problem was not the contract he had with Ken Pitt – that could be resolved. The problem was that he had given too much control to his manager and his record company. As an artist, he needed to spend his time creating and both his management contract with Pitt and his record contract with Mercury prevented this, saddling him with issues and decisions and giving too much control to other parties. What a manager should be doing, said Tony, was to take all the decisions away from the artist, including paying the musicians and the rent and anything else that needed to be done, leaving the artist free to create. Leaning forward, David nodded in agreement. A plan was beginning to emerge.

It was the genesis of the greatest piece of performance art of the twentieth century. David, convinced that he had made a dreadful error in handing too much control to Pitt and Mercury, handed complete control to Tony Defries.

Many tomes about Bowie record that Bowie later rued the fact that the agreement with Defries meant that David had handed his new manager fifty percent of everything he would earn for many years to come – after David alone had paid for the expenses from his half – but it is also almost certain that it was this encounter that led to him having any substantial income to split with a manager at all. Certainly, there was little sign of riches under the patronage of Ken Pitt.

Tony Zanetta told me about that time:

> *I'm not sure if David would have become star because Tony [Defries] was almost a sociopath when it came to money. He didn't care about money. He wanted to make money, but that wasn't his real bit, you know. He could spend and spend. He didn't have to have the money to spend it. Most of us are restricted by that. He said, "I'll figure everything out and at the end of the day, if we make any money, then we'll split it 50/50 after our expenses." So, if you don't have any money or too many prospects, that sounds pretty good. So, they're going to pay your rent. They're gonna take care of all your needs, you know. And they're going to pay for your musicians, so David said, "Yeah, I'll do it." He had nothing to lose.*

And a lot to gain – and he did gain a lot, didn't he? Said Tony:

> *They both did. They won!*

They won by playing the game magnificently. Bowie was to focus on acting the part of a superstar and Defries would bankroll everything and create the mystique.

Cherry Vanilla, the publicist for Defries's company MainMan, was interviewed by Pete Thompson in 2022:

> *We were performing an incredible, unrehearsed improvisation of how to create the world's most famous rock star ... just making it up as we went along. And with David and Defries allowing us both the freedom and authority to do so, it was like the adrenaline high of all time.*

What could be more fitting for a creation like Ziggy than to be made an instant star, simply by deciding to be one and being treated as such – with someone like Tony Defries to foot the bill? That this was a piece of performance art was emphasised by the cast of characters. Before taking his roles in Bowie's entourage, Tony Zanetta was an actor who had appeared in the role of Andy Warhol in Warhol's play *Pork*. He began to get attention from people who treated him as if he was Warhol, although those people were also fully aware that he was not. Z, as he was known, came to realise that it was possible to play a part and be accepted not just as an actor portraying the part effectively but as if he were himself the character. Bowie was beginning to discover the same thing.

As if to emphasise the performative nature of things, Zanetta became tour manager for the Ziggy tour. He explains:

> *Yes, I became the tour manager by default. I went to England just after the Rainbow concert and they did a few dates in England before coming to the US. We get to the hotel – I can't remember which city – and we ended up just sitting in the lobby. And I want to get to my room. So finally ... I didn't know what was going on. I never had this kind of experience, but finally I went to the front desk and asked for the keys and they gave me all the keys. So, I wrote down all the rooms and the numbers and who I gave the keys to. I mean, I wasn't meaning to be the road manager, I just wanted to get to my room. And I just needed to know where everyone was. So, I made a list of who's in what room. But basically, that is what a road manager does, so I basically became the road manager by default. I stepped into it.*

Tony continued in the role and a few weeks later, at the start of the American tour, Defries confirmed, "You'll be the road manager."

"Well, Tony, what is it that I should do?" he asked.

"Oh, gee. Just make sure they find Cleveland," was Defries's response. As Z confirmed in our interview, the bus driver already knew how to get to Cleveland!

It was the most ambitious piece of performance art imaginable. Bowie's career was being run by a lawyer with no experience of managing acts, while his tour was being run by an actor who also was to become president of Defries's management company, MainMan – and the two would be the architects of David's career. The vice-president was Leee Black Childers, photographer and stage manager of *Pork*. Cherry Vanilla, who played the title role in *Pork*, became Bowie's publicist and set about writing a column for teen magazine *Mirabelle* as if she were Bowie (including references to herself in David's voice as "my amazing publicist") and telling stories about what had happened in her own life as if they had happened to David.

So enticing to play the part. Not only was Bowie playing the role of Ziggy Stardust but he had a supporting cast composed literally of actors, no script and the stage was the whole world. Regrettably, sometimes we must live in the "real" world, and when it transpired that David had signed away not only half of all his future earnings but had also agreed to be ultimately responsible for all costs before the remainder was split between himself and his manager, a split with Defries was inevitable.

Eventually, when Bowie had made it, he and Defries realised they didn't need each other any more and Bowie realised that his very substantial earnings were largely going to his manager. It was expensive for Bowie to extricate himself from his contract and Defries ended up with 50% of Bowie's earnings until 1982. It is no coincidence that Bowie released *Let's Dance*, in 1983 – and it would become a massive hit.

* * *

All of this was a long way from everyone's mind when the meeting between David, the Spiders and Defries took place – but it certainly set the scene for how the meeting would go. Defries, to his own mind at least, had made a star. There was no money coming in, but he had bankrolled everything. The band was travelling first class and staying in the best hotels in the world. Bowie had been trying for years to make it and would have been a star no matter who was playing the instrument behind him – the stardom was based on the supreme act of theatre that they had all been producing. To Defries's mind, though, the success coincided with his arrival.

Another view, held by the band, was that the success Bowie had tried for years to attain had now come about because he at last had a solid band of musicians to back him – besides, they resented the fact that other musicians were being paid far more. Both perspectives were correct, but each of the actors in the scene was focused on their own part and not on their fellow players – any actor aware of the Meisner technique knows of the importance of focusing on the other actor rather than themselves.

Mick Ronson was curiously quiet during the meeting; it transpired later that Defries had already been playing divide and conquer by offering Ronson his own solo deal – and promised to make him a star as he had David. Trevor was his usual quiet self. Woody, who had been brought into the band partly because he was regarded as strait-laced and no trouble, was the one who spoke up. Defries now tried to put Woody in his place by telling him that he would rather increase the pay of the roadies than that of Woody and Trevor. They were left in no doubt as to Defries's estimation of their value. Woody countered, "In that case, I'm off the fucking tour. I'm not doing the remaining dates." Woody says he was only partly bluffing. He hoped things would be sorted out and he could continue but, in the absence of a resolution, he was prepared to walk.

Woody must have known that his longer-term future must now be in jeopardy. He turned to Bowie: "What do you think of all this?"

"You're just a fucking backing band. I could have made it with anybody," said Bowie.

In the event, Defries and Bowie couldn't afford to lose key members of the band mid-tour, with the inevitable cancelled dates and the scramble to find, audition and rehearse a replacement, so a settlement was reached for the rest of the tour. Things calmed down and the tour continued a little more happily, although there was, understandably, something of an atmosphere.

As far as the public was concerned, the tour was an absolute triumph and culminated in a show in the heart of the capital at Hammersmith Odeon. Filmmaker D. A. Pennebaker filmed the occasion for posterity and a future cinematic release. Ringo Starr, Mick Jagger and other luminaries were in attendance. Though filmed with only four cameras, all of which seemed to struggle with framing and focus in the lighting conditions, and despite the slightly muffled sound quality, this beautifully captures Bowie as Ziggy at the height of his powers. From opener 'Hang on to Yourself' to 'Rock 'n' Roll Suicide' the show is a tour de force. The set list is beautifully designed, starting with "here we go" rockers 'Hang on to Yourself', 'Ziggy Stardust' and 'Watch that Man' before slowing things with the ethereal and soaring 'Wild Eyed Boy from Freecloud', then segueing into two singalong numbers 'All the Young Dudes' and 'Oh! You Pretty Things' and thence into the blistering 'Moonage Daydream' – by which point the crowd had already been on a roller-coaster journey and were utterly enthralled. Now the wistful 'Changes' and old favourite 'Space Oddity' further showed the breadth and depth of Bowie's back catalogue. Ten songs in, Bowie played his first cover, the extraordinary Jacques Brel song 'My Death'. The audience is spellbound as Bowie concludes:

> But whatever lies behind the door
> There is nothing much to do
> Angel or devil, I don't care
> For in front of that door, there is…

At which point Bowie pauses for a split second and, before he is able to sing the final word *you*, an audience member yells, "ME!" Catching on quickly, dozens or hundreds more shout the same, whereupon Bowie simply says: "Thank you" and stands to leave the stage. An astonishing moment.

To be joined for encores by Jeff Beck, an idol of Ronson's, was confirmation of the status that Bowie had attained on this tour. His performance, missing at Beck's request from the film and subsequent album, was shown beautifully restored in Brett Morgen's 2022 film *Moonage Daydream* and in the rereleased version of Pennebaker's film in 2023.

As Beck left the stage, Bowie stepped up to the microphone. What was to come was to be a complete surprise to many of the key players. It has become *de rigueur* to say that Bowie "killed" Ziggy. Perhaps he did, in a sense. Layers of artifice had simply become too much for David, or perhaps anyone, to manage. Where did Ziggy start and Bowie end? Where did Bowie end and David Jones start? Indeed, even the name "David" was erased from 1973's *Pin Ups* album and 1974's *Diamond Dogs*, leaving "Bowie" as the sole designation.

After thanking a number of people, the bombshell was dropped: "Of all the shows on this tour, this particular show will remain with us the longest because not only is it – not only is the last show of the tour but it's the last show that we will ever do." Whereupon Woody and Trevor looked around wondering what they'd just heard and how significant it might be. Guitarist John "Hutch' Hutchinson launched into the strummed acoustic chords of 'Rock 'n' Roll Suicide' and the audience went even more wild.

Mick Ronson had known about the plan in advance, but Trevor and Woody were in the dark – partly because Tony Defries feared that, having threatened to leave the tour once, they might do so again if they got wind of the plot. Two days later, it was Woody's wedding day – he had proposed to his girlfriend June during the tour. Mike Garson married them. Bowie and Ronson were invited but didn't attend. Instead, Woody received a call from Tony Defries on the day of the wedding to say that his services were no longer required by Bowie and – just to be sure Woody was in no doubt as to his perceived worth – that he was to be replaced by a drum machine.

In the coming months, Bowie would in fact continue with the Ziggy guise, recording an album of covers, *Pin Ups*, with Ronson and Bolder and with Aynsley Dunbar on drums. In October, he appeared in Ziggy guise in a made-for-TV performance that he dubbed *The 1980 Floor Show*, for American TV show *Midnight Special*, again with both Bolder and Ronson, but that was the end of the road for the remaining Spiders. For his next record of original material, Bowie dispensed with his former band entirely – and with his producer Ken Scott, choosing instead to handle production entirely alone and to play almost all the guitar on the album too. With Ronson's string arrangement skills absent, Tony Visconti returned to fill the void with string arrangements on one track and to contribute his mixing skills.

The album, *Diamond Dogs*, is regarded as one of his greatest among fans and critics. It's the album that gave us the classily insistent riffage of 'Rebel Rebel' for God's sake. And Bowie still retained his Ziggy mullet. However, the Ziggy project was over. This was both an extension of the basic idea taken to its natural apocalyptic extreme and a new beginning. While many regard the *Diamond Dogs* era as a time in which Bowie portrayed a new character, Halloween Jack, this was entirely different from the Ziggy Stardust and Aladdin Sane characters which were lived to the full by Bowie.

The Ziggy period will always stand as a pivotal time in Bowie's career and in popular music as a whole. To have invented a character, lived it fully on stage and off, and created a global phenomenon in the way that he did was both audacious and unprecedented. In a book such as this, based around dozens of *Sliding Doors* moments, any of which could have sent Bowie's career in another direction, the arrival of Mick Ronson may be the most impactful.

He took it all too far – but boy, could he play guitar.

Chapter 3
THE SUPERMEN

The departure of Mick Ronson meant that Bowie needed not only a new guitar player but also a string arranger – and because of the coinciding break with Ken Scott, Bowie needed a producer too. His old friend Tony Visconti had both skills.

Meeting Tony Visconti for the first time was quite a moment for me. After all, he was the producer of albums spanning from 1969's *Space Oddity* album to 2016's *Blackstar* as well as timeless songs by T. Rex, Thin Lizzy, the Boomtown Rats and many others. His sonic visions, if you'll excuse the mixed metaphor, had shaped the music landscape of several generations, but particularly the glam era.

My first meeting with Tony happened before the *Blackstar* album was released and while Bowie was still alive. I attended a gig in June 2015 by Tony's band, Holy Holy, which also included Woody Woodmansey, Bowie's drummer from 1970 until 1973, Glenn Gregory from Heaven 17 and other luminaries. They were an incredibly powerful band playing from Bowie's album *The Man Who Sold the World* – a work I had been intimately familiar with for decades, but the performance that night made me listen anew. I remember saying that I couldn't understand why it wasn't regarded as Bowie's greatest classic. It wasn't – and isn't – but it seemed that way then. In the light of day, of course, I realise it's because he produced so many other classics – many of which surpassed this 1970 effort. Such is the power of live performance.

In 1970, after the album was released, the band broke up. As we have seen, the newly married Bowie had become somewhat detached during the making of the album and Tony had decided to focus his energies on Marc Bolan, who seemed much more enthusiastic about writing and recording. Decades later, when Bowie asked the reason for the tour, Tony said, "because we didn't tour it at the time" – and David seemed content with that response.

Tony moved from Brooklyn to London at the moment when the city was said to be in full swing – but in fact he found it rather bewildering. The TV went black before midnight, and there were only three channels; houses and apartments had baths but not showers; and the currency, with 240 pence per pound, along with farthings, sixpences, shillings, florins and half-crowns, was unfathomable. Most people seemed to have straight jobs and short hair and Tony was routinely sneered at for his longer hair. The Swinging London that he hoped to find was limited to one or two streets. Through his association with producer Denny Cordell, he arrived in London to record Georgie Fame and went on to work with Tyrannosaurus Rex on the album *My People Were Fair and Had Sky in Their Hair... But Now They're Content to Wear Stars on Their Brows*, a majestic title that their American label shortened to *Tyrannosaurus Rex: A Beginning*.

On Monday, 24 July 1967, David Platz of Essex Music

contacted Ken Pitt, Bowie's then manager, to tell him about Tony, who he knew was now working with Denny Cordell. Pitt then met with Tony to discuss working with Bowie. As Kevin Cann reports, Pitt said that "David was excited and said, 'ring me as soon as you can, I'll be sitting by the phone." Meanwhile, David Platz called young Tony into his office and said – condescendingly according to Tony – "You seem to have a talent for working with weird acts", and played him a recording of *David Bowie*. "This is an album made by a writer I've been working with for some time," he said. "We were hoping he'd be right for musical theatre but he's become something quite different since he's made this record." Tony was intrigued and felt he had the subtle phrasing of a far more seasoned performer than his years would suggest.

Quoting Tony Visconti, biographer David Buckley takes up the story: "I sat there amused by the eclectic styles of the singer. There was a quantum leap of styles between 'The Laughing Gnome' and 'When I Live My Dream'. I think my comment was, 'This guy's all over the place!'" Platz found this amusing but added that Bowie was looking for a producer to guide him in a more straightforward direction. After the meeting, David emerged from the back office where he had been waiting nervously.

The pair were introduced and hit it off immediately, talking about Buddhism, world cinema and little-known recordings and then going to the cinema to see the Roman Polanski film *Knife in the Water*. Clearly, a promising start to their relationship.

If we're looking for those *Sliding Doors* moments when a single moment influenced an entire career, then this must surely be a prominent one. The partnership between David

Bowie and Tony Visconti extends to some 16 albums and is one of the most prolific and influential in rock history.

As Buckley points out, Bowie was at this point, on the cusp between the "cool" world of popular music and the "legit" sphere of theatrical tradition, as exemplified by Pitt, who had poured his considerable efforts into establishing Bowie as a traditional entertainer. Tony offered a different path – that of a more experimental and innovative artist.

A plan to have George Martin produce Bowie's next album – released as *David Bowie* but later rereleased and redubbed *Space Oddity* to avoid confusion with Bowie's previous eponymous LP – went unrealised when Martin passed on the opportunity. Such was Kenneth Pitt's belief in Bowie that he wrote in his diary, "George Martin is fallible". Instead, Tony Visconti was asked to act as producer.

We know that it was Tony who first realised that Bowie needed a stable band of peers – not a rotating cast of ragamuffins, drifters and dreamers that he'd had previously, but equally not 50-year-old, technically proficient session players.

Tony told Dylan Jones, "What we tried for the first album – the *Space Oddity* album which was not quite successful, but wasn't bad – was that he needed a band." This was to prove prophetic and the ongoing quest for a steady band would become a theme. Tony continues, "So I hired a band that I was working with called Junior's Eyes. They were all David's age and really great musicians and they made the album."

This, however, was not quite the band he required. "He needed to drop that twelve-string for a bit and we needed to find a powerhouse band for him," Tony concludes.

The musicians that Tony brought in from Junior's Eyes

were guitarists Mick Wayne and Tim Renwick, bass player John "Honk" Lodge, and drummer John Cambridge. Also playing were the then unknown Rick Wakeman on Mellotron, while Herbie Flowers played some bass, as did Visconti himself. Keith Christmas, Bowie's friend from the Beckenham Arts Lab that David jointly ran, also played some guitar. Terry Cox played some drums and Benny Marshall from Junior's Eyes, whose vocals were not needed, played harmonica.

Bowie would need a stable band as a platform towards his eventual success and this was a step in the right direction but perhaps not quite the breakthrough everyone was aiming for. He now had an embryonic nucleus of a band but had yet to shake off the commune-style approach that had grown for his involvement with the Beckenham Arts Lab and the life that went with his Haddon Hall existence, with its ever-changing *dramatis personae*. But Tony was right – Bowie did need to exist within a tight unit to make progress – it's just that this wasn't quite it yet.

* * *

He was disappointed that his new friend Tony decided to pass on the production of the title track of the album. The song was slated to be recorded first and rush-released as a single to coincide with the 1969 moonshot, but as described earlier Tony regarded it as a novelty song and declined to be involved. "It's not a David Bowie song. It's 'Ernie the Milkman'," is how he put it. Author Chris O'Leary insists that Tony was right:

> *In hock to the Bee Gees' death bubblegum 'New York Mining Disaster' and similar in tone to Zager and Evans'*

> *'In the Year 2525,' 'Space Oddity' is a gimmicky folk song in extravagant garb.*

As Bowie said, you may adopt another point of view. Now that 'Space Oddity' – from a distance of over half a century – is regarded as Bowie's first classic, we struggle to hear the song like those hearing it for the first time in 1969, but it must have seemed out of step with his other material at the time. Elsewhere on the album we have the surreal hippy reflection of 'Memory of a Free Festival'; the plaintive yearning of 'Letter to Hermione'; prophesy mixed with fantasy in 'Wild Eyed Boy from Freecloud', along with familiar Bowie themes such as isolation and human interaction with higher beings; and what must have felt like his magnum opus, 'Cygnet Committee', in which Bowie or his narrator admonishes the hippy movement for falling into the same materialist traps as all previous counterculture efforts. The album is an eclectic mix of styles and messages. The inclusion of a novelty song tied – in what may have seemed like an opportunist gimmick – to the moon landing and to the popular film *2001: A Space Odyssey* proved too much for Tony. He passed production duties on to engineer Gus Dudgeon, who took on the task with gusto, mapping out the various starting points of each section of instrumentation on the walls of the studio – Trident in London.

Fascinated as I always am with the way things were and the way they might have been, I asked Tony in 2017 about his decision to hand over production. Here's how it went:

> *NS: Gus Dudgeon's production of the song 'Space Oddity' seems to follow Bowie's demo very closely. You passed on producing the song, but do you think it would have been*

very different if you had recorded it with him? Might we have a very different 'Space Oddity' if you'd produced it?

TV: If I really liked the song, which I do now, I would've followed the demo too, but it's hard to say. I gave Rick Wakeman his start as a session guy and introduced him to Gus, but Gus came up with the incredible Paul Buckmaster, the cellist on the very bare B-side 'Wild Eyed Boy from Freecloud', to arrange the song. Gus was a better engineer than I was at the time; he did a brilliant job. I think I came into my own as an engineer when David and I rerecorded 'Memory of a Free Festival' with Mick Ronson on guitar and Ralph Mace on Moog. I love that recording; it sounds great and it's a great arrangement too, if I might blow my own horn.

In any event, Gus produced it and, as Tony readily says, did a very fine job indeed. In fact, given Gus' superior engineering ability at the time, the decision by Tony to allow Dudgeon to handle the production may have been a significant factor in bringing about Bowie's first hit.

While I regard the album as the first in a string of classics stretching throughout the decade ahead, many Bowie fans do not, and date his purple period from the subsequent *The Man Who Sold the World*. However, 'Space Oddity' demonstrates a huge leap forward from Bowie's first album, just two years earlier.

Until this point, David's father, John, had guided David's career. John saw to it that David had good advice and avoided some of the financial pitfalls that he knew often befell young artists. When John unexpectedly died from a pulmonary infection, the still young David was deeply affected. Although one might expect that he would look to his manager Ken Pitt as a steadying influence at this point, it was in fact to his younger friends that he turned.

Pitt's background in musical theatre, music hall and 'legit' performance had started to feel at odds with the counterculture existence that David had built at Haddon Hall. When, barely a month after the loss of his father, 'Space Oddity' became a top five hit, David was confused and, according to Pitt, in the 'depths of despair', simultaneously dealing with grief and success and also returning to his home at Haddon Hall, where the occupants were anti -success and anti-materialist.

It was a confusing time for a young performer who had been hungry for success. He couldn't continue his hippy-style existence and be a successful pop star: the Haddon Hall vibe suited him as an aspiring folkie muso but not as a burgeoning singer-songwriter poised to take his place on the world stage. Involving Uncle Tom Cobley and all was an approach fostered at Haddon Hall and which Visconti could see was hampering Bowie from finding the tight-knit, pared back band that he needed to move forward. However, it would be at least another two years before Bowie made the break. Bowie's subsequent singles flopped, easing things at Haddon Hall. He and Angie continued to live in the flat within the Victorian mansion, later with their young son Duncan Zowie. And though it did not offer the stability he needed, Haddon Hall would become the birthplace of the Spiders from Mars, bringing together Mick Ronson, Woody Woodmansey and Trevor Bolder to form the tight unit that Tony knew was needed.

The moment of the birth of glam is somewhat disputed. Prior to the Roundhouse gig in which Bowie's Hype had performed as characters in costume, Marc Bolan had appeared on *Top of the Pops* with glitter beneath his eyes. Which of these moments signals the birth of glam rock is up to the observer to decide. Perhaps it depends on whether you regard glam rock as being about glitter and sparkle or about portraying a character. Perhaps it depends on whether you're a bigger fan of Bowie or Bolan. Or perhaps it doesn't matter very much. In any case, Tony Visconti, the collaborator and producer of both, brought together glam's two early protagonists on 'The Prettiest Star' – Bowie's follow-up to 'Space Oddity'. David must have liked the song as he rerecorded it for *Aladdin Sane,* but the original version failed to hit the public mood in the way that 'Space Oddity' had and sank without trace. The recording session with Marc Bolan went well, though it was marred by the reaction of his wife June. Approaching Bowie at the end of the session, she declared that Marc was a star in his own right and far too good to be playing on the likes of a David Bowie song, leaving David and Tony somewhat aghast and an embarrassed Bolan leaving without a word.

As Tony says in his autobiography, Bolan's downfall was that he refused to change. Having found a formula that worked, he stuck to it with diminishing returns and refused to grow as an artist, always insisting on recording one more similar album "for the kids", despite the fact that the kids' interests were changing and that they were no longer kids in any case. Three years is a long time in rock 'n' roll. As we've seen, Bowie's longevity as an artist lay in his propensity to take a completely new and unexpected direction and surprise and intrigue his audience.

The next album he made, *The Man Who Sold the World*, is regarded by many fans as Bowie's first classic. Tony's production ability had improved through practice, and the solid band of Mick Ronson, Woody Woodmansey and himself provided the tight unit that enabled Bowie to grow and flourish as an artist. That Bowie was able to leave the band to work up the songs and sort out the arrangements while he spent time with Angie or, indeed, sleeping, is testament to the stability of the structure now supporting David.

However, the album *The Man Who Sold the World* was to be Tony's last with Bowie for a while. As already described, there was no tour to support the album, no single taken from it to promote sales. Essentially, the band broke up and Visconti decided to put his efforts into T. Rex because Marc Bolan was experiencing a level of success and a far better work ethic.

Tony produced a slew of successful singles and albums for Bolan while simultaneously keeping an eye on Bowie's career progression. On hearing *Hunky Dory* he felt a small pang of envy. Where were these great songs when he was producing Bowie? The years that Visconti was away were indeed good to Bowie. Tony Defries and MainMan cast their incredible spells over their man and the world around him, creating the aura required to make the world believe that Bowie was a superstar while Bowie himself created the object of the mystique, the Ziggy Stardust character. After the incredible success of *Hunky Dory's* follow-up, *The Rise and Fall of Ziggy Stardust and the Spiders from Mars*, and its successor, *Aladdin Sane*, Bowie had famously retired from live performance, recorded a covers album, *Pin Ups,* and dismissed the remaining members of his core band – and now it was time to record a new album.

This time, there was no Ken Scott to co-produce, no Ronson or Visconti to do string arrangements, not even a steady band to rely on. In 1969, he had needed a solid platform of talented musicians, arrangers and producers to launch his success. He had parted from Tony Visconti in 1970 feeling he needed more control, and now he had taken things even more steps further, leaving the task of making the next album as much as possible to himself. He, not Ronson, would play the guitar. He, not Visconti or Scott, would produce – alone. Bowie was determined to prove that his success was down to his own talents and abilities, not just to his talent for surrounding himself with the right people. He was about to try to prove that he was not simply the collector that he had proclaimed himself, drawing the best out of others; he wanted to prove his mettle alone. To claim that *Diamond Dogs* was his first solo album would be going too far, but not by much.

This did not mean he had abandoned the idea of gathering ideas, assembling influences and combining them in interesting ways. Ever the disparate artist, Bowie had been working up a musical stage show based on George Orwell's *Nineteen Eighty-Four* but had failed to secure the rights from the writer's widow, so instead he repurposed the songs for the album, many of which lift phrases directly from the book. '1984', 'We are the Dead' and 'Big Brother' are the most immediately recognisable examples.

Decades later, Bowie reflected on this: "I knew that the guitar playing had to be more than okay," he said, clearly feeling the weight of responsibility on his shoulders. It was the only time in his life he actually did any guitar practice. Bowie had initially announced that he would be playing every instrument himself. In the event, Mike Garson played piano and Aynsley Dunbar the drums, while Herbie Flowers, veteran of the *Space Oddity* sessions, handled the bass. Bowie did play almost all of the guitars, however (supplemented by Alan Parker who played on '1984' and a little on 'Rebel Rebel') plus all the synthesizers and saxophone. Bowie took a notably autocratic approach to his production, with Mike Garson saying that he felt more like a session musician than a part of a band – a notable change of emphasis as compared with, say, *Aladdin Sane*, on which Mike was given a large degree of freedom to create.

So Tony Visconti was surprised, to say the least, when he received a phone call during the making of the album. Initially, Bowie had called in the middle of the night wishing to reconnect and promising to meet soon, but neither men then made contact for several months until Bowie called again. He had been working on mixing the album alongside Keith Harwood but was not happy with the results. At this point, Bowie didn't go so far as to ask Tony to mix it but requested advice on a good studio to use to get the results he required. Serendipitously, Visconti, with the benefit of a 1 per cent royalty on T. Rex's hit records, had bought a house in London with his wife Mary Hopkin, the lower floor of which was given over entirely to a photographic studio. What better place for a music producer to build his own studio? Everything fell into place. Mary no longer enjoyed performing live but did wish to continue a recording career, and Tony's accountant had advised that if he didn't put the money into a project he would have to pay it in tax, so the decision was easy to make.

The one drawback was that the studio was barely ready to be used. Although the mixing desk and other hardware was in place, there was as yet no furniture, so the two old friends rekindled their relationship mixing the *Diamond Dogs* album while sitting on two builders' saw benches.

Within a few days, a Habitat van drew up outside with all the furniture the studio needed – a gift from David, which must have helped seal their renewed relationship. Pleased though he was with the gesture, Tony had one question: "Why a dining room set?"

Bowie explained that they were going to have their food delivered during the mixing process, and there followed a highly civilised few weeks during which the pair enjoyed food from the finest restaurants along with a few glasses of good claret.

The album itself captured the zeitgeist perfectly once again, which seems odd for an album based on a 25-year-old dystopian novel that imagines a future in which society has broken down, institutions have fallen and disorder reigns. However, Bowie rendered his vision against a UK backdrop – back in the real world – of three-day working weeks, power cuts, fuel shortage and uncollected refuse accumulating on the streets, bringing public health scares. Bowie was, as ever, simply taking events from his immediate environment, extending them to their extreme but logical conclusion, and showing the world what lay ahead on its current path.

In the event, the album made use of Keith Harwood's previous mixes of 'Rebel Rebel', 'Rock 'n' Roll With Me' and 'We Are The Dead', while Visconti was also called on to arrange the strings for '1984'. His use of the then new Eventide Digital Delay is much in evidence and lends the album much of its distinctiveness. There was and remains little like *Diamond Dogs*, despite its influence on the coming punk movement. Bowie must have felt vindicated at producing the album alone and playing so many of the instruments, even if he did call on Tony for help with the mixing.

As ever with Bowie's albums, there are tracks which hint to the future direction that Bowie will take, and the heavily treated wah-wah guitars strongly point towards the Philadelphia-influenced soul and funk vibes that he was now starting to embrace. That move, physical as well as metaphorical, would signal the end of Bowie's relationship with anything that could be described as "rock" for many years to come. As he himself said in 1975, "People really needed rock 'n' roll… but it's become one more whirling deity, going round that never-decreasing circle." Further, he said, "rock 'n' roll is just a toothless old woman." In the excellent *Bowie: Album by Album*, Paolo Hewitt points out that at this time:

> *The Beatles are finished; the Stones have been hijacked by Keith's addictions and Mick's avarice; Led Zeppelin are running out of steam; The Faces have split up and all the glam rock bands are finished. There are some bands still creating vital sounds – Dr Feelgood, Thin Lizzy, Graham Parker – but not enough for the period to qualify as a golden age.*

Thank God Bowie changed tack when he did.

His appearance on *Diamond Dogs* is extremely Ziggy-esque and prompted some to wonder why, when Bowie had supposedly killed (or perhaps retired) Ziggy, he was so in evidence for two more albums. The answer, of course, is that the killing of Ziggy is more of a retrospective idea than a contemporary one. Indeed, the character that he had lived so completely was difficult for him to shake off – that was evident not only in the way that Bowie now acted every bit the superstar in accordance with Defries' master plan, refusing interviews and publicly doing little for himself and overtly expecting his needs to be met on demand. Furthermore, the potential loss of self was emphasised by the eradication of the last vestige of his birth name. We've seen that for *Pin Ups* and *Diamond Dogs* he would be billed only as Bowie. Clearly, it was harder to shake the character than he had hoped.

The following tour is fabled in Bowie history, and was a hugely ambitious undertaking. Fortunately, it seems there was little or no negative backlash to his return to stage less than a year after he'd proclaimed the show at Hammersmith to be "the last show that we will ever do." Perhaps it was now at least partly understood that it was the Ziggy character who was speaking rather than the artist himself. That Bowie had described it as the last show that *we* would ever do – leaving the *I* free to continue. Or perhaps people took the view that this new highly elaborate Diamond Dogs show couldn't be regarded as a rock 'n' roll gig anyway. Nothing this elaborate had been seen in rock circles to date. The set, costing a quarter of a million dollars, was based partly on German expressionist films such as Fritz Lang's groundbreaking 1927 dystopian film *Metropolis,* in which workers feature as cogs in the industrial machine that keeps the privileged in luxury away from vastly overpopulated cities, and the 1920 film *The Cabinet of Dr. Caligari* in which a hypnotist uses a somnambulist to commit murders.

In Bowie's set, designed by Mark Ravitz, huge skyscrapers rose from the sides of the stage flanking a central bridge against a backdrop the urban decay of Hunger City. The show was a highly choreographed mixture of dance, drama, mime and song. Performers were threatened with fines if they ad-libbed a line or move that might disrupt the show. This was Bowie artifice taken to its extreme but logical conclusion – the antithesis of what rock had become in the '60s when long onstage improvised jams had become the norm and the artist's role was to express themselves in the moment. This was contemporary art, skilfully blurring the lines between art forms while also presenting a show choreographed meticulously by Toni Basil.

What was also clear was that previously exaggerated rumours of Ziggy's retirement had come true. The Ziggy haircut and kimonos that were so in evidence in the audience were nowhere to be seen on the stage, replaced with a shorter, swept-back red with blond streaks and a rather more conventional wardrobe.

Notoriously, the show did not make it to the UK – it was far too expensive and the technicalities rendered it difficult to operate. On one memorable occasion, a seat which extended from the stage over the audience got stuck mid song leaving Bowie to perform a number of songs from on high before he could be retrieved. On another occasion, the driver of the lorry moving the scenery and lighting was stung by a wasp, causing him to crash into a ditch. The show that evening went ahead despite thoughts of cancellation and was regarded as a very special performance – perhaps the best of the tour.

The tour itself holds an exalted place in Bowie history for two reasons: its theatricality and the fact that it was never properly filmed. Such is the mystique of the tour that even today, Bowie fans who know the answer still optimistically ask those in the know if a film will ever come to light. Sadly, it won't – it's not like a lost *Top of the Pops* performance that has been wiped from the BBC archives but may be found via a private copy, the tour was simply never filmed. Sound recordings were made and released, most notably the double album *David Live*, on which the great contrast between the 'live' sound of the tour and the album are highly evident. Whereas the album has a raw quality that has led many to regard it as proto punk, Bowie hired highly competent professional musicians for the tour, giving a slick smooth vibe with all the rough edges smoothed out. Seemingly truly back in the fold now, Tony Visconti produced the album.

The Diamond Dogs tour closed on 20 July 1974 and when it resumed in September it had morphed into the Soul tour / the Philly Dogs tour. Many of the musicians had left and new ones been appointed in their place, and the set list included a number of songs that Bowie had recorded for a new album – namely 'Can You Hear Me?', 'Somebody Up There Likes Me', 'Win', and 'Young Americans'. In the control booth co-producing once again was Bowie's old friend, Tony Visconti. Having proved to himself that that he could, if not go it alone, at least make a great album without feeling that the influence of a collaborator was too great, Bowie was now a little more relaxed about collaborating with an old partner.

* * *

The preface to this book begins with Carlos Alomar on the stage, wowing the crowd at Wembley. To get to know him and Robin Clark, his wife who sang on *Young Americans*, has been remarkable. As well as being a master guitarist, Carlos is a storyteller who can hold an audience in the palm of his hand. When I jointly curated an international convention of Bowie alumni in Liverpool, he was the perfect choice.

That's also why we asked him to return for a second year in New York. On the night before the convention, we met for drinks and Carlos was erudite and thought-provoking. As he stood up, he said, "That's what talking with Carlos Alomar is like. Imagine what it's like when Carlos Alomar is talking with David Bowie!"

Carlos Alomar's journey to becoming David Bowie's guitarist from 1974 until 2003 – with some breaks – has its genesis in the adoption of a new persona. With the Ziggy character and its successors discarded, Bowie began to immerse himself in the 'plastic soul' and funk of 1974 Philadelphia. He was soon to discover Carlos Alomar, who had the chops for this in spades and was an integral part of Bowie's new guise as a funk and soul man. Bowie's talent for collecting ideas and the right people never showed itself more clearly and Carlos became central to Bowie's musical world for decades to come.

What Bowie may have been less aware of at the time was his own need not only for a musician and foil but also, as his paranoia and drug use spiralled, for a friend. It was during the Ziggy Stardust period that David had begun overindulging in cocaine, becoming ever more distant from the band and his friends. Drummer Woody Woodmansey recalls that Bowie's remoteness was often put down to the changes that success brings because at this point the drug-taking was rather clandestine.

By the time of the Diamond Dogs tour, all that had changed. Bowie had created the album more or less alone, playing all the guitars himself, so he needed someone else for the tour. He contacted Keith Christmas, who had played on the *Space Oddity* album. Christmas flew out to New York but found Bowie overindulging in cocaine and amyl nitrate – and passed. As Nicholas Pegg brilliantly put it, "*Diamond Dogs* was not for Christmas."

One person who did sign on at this time, however, was Michael Kamen. Bowie had seen a Kamen ballet, *Rodin, Mis En Vie*, which was based on the sculptor Auguste Rodin. Bowie met Kamen afterwards and asked him to be his musical director and keyboard player. During that same month, April 1974, David began to frequent Harlem's Apollo: he had been somewhat obsessed with James Brown's *Live at the Apollo* since its release a decade earlier and the venue itself held a special status for him. There, one Carlos Alomar was a member of the house band. The two had already met at RCA's studios on Sixth Avenue, where Lulu was recording David's song 'Can You Hear Me?, and Alomar was playing guitar.

In August 1974, Bowie went to Philadelphia to record the album that would become *Young Americans*. He was obsessed at the time with all things Black – including Black women, notes Ava Cherry drily, the singer whose career he had promised to help launch. She couldn't pin him down, though, so Tony Defries asked Michael Kamen to help and he linked her up with Sigma Sound Studios in North 12th Street. It was an area that was run-down, but artists such as the O'Jays, the Stylistics and the Spinners recorded there, and it had the right vibe. Ava recorded David's 'Sweet Thing' there and when Bowie dropped by to see how things were going, he was impressed with the facilities and wanted to use their resident group, MFSB, for his album. They were unavailable, so he contacted a range of Black musicians he had encountered in New York, including Carlos Alomar.

At the after-party following a gig by Todd Rundgren at Carnegie Hall on 19 April, Bowie told journalists that he had "found a really incredible black guy called Carlos". Carlos is in fact Puerto Rican. Either way, he was earning more than $800 per session at this time and was consequently unmoved by the offer that Bowie's manager Tony Defries made – $250 per week. The negotiations went no further at this point, but Bowie remained infatuated. The first part of the Diamond Dogs tour, in June and July 1974, went ahead with another future Bowie stalwart guitarist, Earl Slick, making an early appearance.

The events that led to Carlos eventually joining the tour had an uncanny familiarity. Like the Ziggy Stardust tour, the Diamond Dogs tour ended with musicians threatening not to play and subsequently leaving the fold due to a disagreement about money. Seeing extra microphones and other equipment set up at a show at the Tower Theater, Upper Darby, Philadelphia, the band quickly deduced that a live recording was being made. They had not been informed and their contracts forbade such recordings unless payment of $5000 per musician was paid. Bassist Herbie Flowers confronted David and the band refused to play unless they were paid. Tony Defries offered $470 – the union rate – which was flatly rejected. Eventually, the $5000 fee was agreed and the band went on, but relations were soured and many musicians left when the first leg of the tour concluded at Madison Square Garden on 20 July 1974. After staying in town for a week and seeing the Jackson 5 perform at the same venue, Bowie headed to Philadelphia to record *Young Americans* at Sigma Sound Studios, commencing on 8 August.

Around this time, and to Alomar's surprise, he received a call. "You don't expect to receive a call from a guy who's been trying to hook up with you for a couple of albums,"

Alomar remarked, but this time a deal was struck and Bowie's "terrific black guy" was employed as a guitarist on the album and for the September–December legs of the ongoing tour.

Throughout his career, Bowie was a master at absorbing the zeitgeist, as well as the vibe of his immediate environment, and never more so than in 1974, when he famously told Alan Yentob that he was like a fly that he saw in his milk: "I couldn't help but soak it up." He now had the perfect guide, and along with Carlos he visited local clubs soaking up various forms of Black music, much of which would emerge on the heavily funk- and soul-influenced album that followed.

As can be seen from the Alan Yentob film *Cracked Actor*, and from the snippets of the tour that were filmed, Bowie was very pale and thin at this time. Producer Tony Visconti recalls arriving in town on 11 August, three days after sessions had begun and running straight to the studio, arriving in the early evening. David, who was now sleeping in the daytime, arrived at midnight and they immediately recorded 'Young Americans'.

Carlos Alomar could hardly have been more influential upon Bowie and his career trajectory at this time. Bowie had changed course many times in his career at this point, but this was the first to have occurred since he had hit his stride and found success with Ziggy Stardust in the glam rock genre. Reductive though we may feel these genre labels to be, each of the albums he had produced post Ziggy – *Aladdin Sane*, *Pin Ups*, *Diamond Dogs* – can be identified with that genre. The pre-Ziggy *Hunky Dory*, often labelled as a folk album, can certainly be regarded as proto-glam in part. But Bowie didn't stick to the formula. This was the first of Bowie's masterstrokes which earned him the description of *chameleon*. Before glam sunk, Bowie jumped ship and completely reinvented himself as a purveyor of 'plastic' soul, whilst less adaptable artists such as his frenemy Marc Bolan, Mott the Hoople, and Sweet floundered.

In Carlos he had a guide who was heavily steeped in soul and funk, having not only played in the house band at the famed Apollo backing the likes of Chuck Berry but also having toured for eight months with James Brown. Bowie now set about making use of his new partner and applying what he had learned. Memorably, the *Cracked Actor* film shows Bowie directing a group of Black vocalists – including Carlos's wife Robin Clark and a pre-fame Luther Vandross – through the complex vocal arrangements of the song 'Right' while sniffing and making slightly embarrassed comments about his methods.

In 1974, Bowie seemed like an alien creature indeed. Carlos described him to biographer Dylan Jones as the whitest guy he had ever seen. He was possibly one of the thinnest too with red hair and a pasty pallor. In 2022, Carlos kindly agreed to speak at a Bowie convention that I was curating in Liverpool, and I can attest that Carlos is one of the friendliest and most engaging people one could hope to meet – and it was certainly timely that he met Bowie at a time when the singer needed a friend. Never one to mince words, Carlos said to Bowie: "You look like shit. You need to eat some fucking food!" and promptly invited him for dinner with himself and Robin. "We were just being kind, humble, neighbourly and fair," he now says. David certainly needed a friend – and a meal!

In addition to exposing Bowie to the Black music that so influenced him at this time, Carlos also assembled a large number of the musicians who performed on the album. In addition to the backing singers, he brought in bass players Emir Ksasan and Willie Weeks, drummers Andy Newmark and Dennis Davis. Was this a one-sided affair in which Bowie took advantage of Carlos's abilities and connections? Not a bit of it. When asked if Bowie was a genius, he quickly responds: "Yes!" and talks of looking up to the singer. But he also looked at David as a friend. "He chose to live next to me. He invited me into his life – I let him in. He took Nile Rodgers, Luther Vandross, all my contacts. All my phone book is in David Bowie's hands. Yes, we were friends."

The relationship between these two highly creative people grew through the making of *Young Americans*, subsequent albums and related tours – and like all the subjects in the chapters of this book, Carlos can rightly claim that Bowie's career would have been radically different without his influence. One example of this led to Bowie's first US number one hit single. Bowie appeared on *The Dick Cavett Show* performing a cover version of 'Foot Stompin'' by The Flares, a heavy funk number in keeping with David's then current preoccupation, which also benefitted from a repetitive funky original guitar lick from Carlos. The song was played on tour but sounded ordinary in the studio. The hypnotic, unresolved riff by Carlos Alomar was far too good to be used on a cover of another artist's song, so Bowie, in keeping with his penchant for absorption and repurposing, started to take pieces from the song and arrange them in a much more stripped-back way to begin to form a new piece.

Bowie had become friendly with John Lennon in LA in 1974 and now, in January 1975, while deep into the second set of sessions for *Young Americans,* he heard that Lennon was in New York and, ever the collector and no doubt keen to have an artist of Lennon's stature on his album, invited him to the studio to assist with Bowie's cover of 'Across the Universe'. John added some rhythm guitar and on hearing the Carlos riff, picked up one of Carlos's guitars and played some acoustic guitar. Claims that the song was based on 'Shame Shame Shame' by Shirley & Company in Tony Zanetta's book *Stardust* seem mistaken, and Bowie himself said in 1980 that Lennon had repeatedly sung the word *aim* which morphed into Bowie's treatise on the ills of his current lifestyle and became 'Fame'. At this point the negative aspects of the life of a celebrity weighed somewhat heavily on him, relatively new to its realities. As both Nicholas Pegg and David Buckley point out, the bitter disillusionment shown in this track stands in stark contrast to the *Ziggy Stardust* song 'Star', in which Bowie dreams wistfully about the same trappings of fame that he now appears to feel great antipathy towards. Lennon has also said that the song was based on a Stevie Wonder middle eight. In a supreme example of Bowie's nature as a collector, the combination of Lennon, Alomar, Wonder and Bowie produced Bowie's first visit to the top of the US charts.

Elsewhere on the album, a Luther Vandross original was repurposed to become 'Fascination'. It may be tempting to conclude that the cocaine-filled Bowie, disillusioned with fame and at a creative nadir, was forced to magpie and repurpose ideas from friends and other artists to produce an album, managing only eight tracks, but this is an example of Bowie doing what he always did throughout his career – absorbing and redirecting ideas from around him to create something entirely new and fresh. Much later he would use an original song by his guitarist Kevin Armstrong as the basis for the title track from his *1. Outside* album. Earlier, he had based 'Life on Mars?' on the original version of 'My Way' after his lyrics for the song were rejected. There are many, many more examples. Bowie's mastery, as we have seen, often lay not in absolute originality but in absorbing ideas and recycling them into something greater than the source material.

The rhythm section assembled for the later session of the album – Alomar and Dennis Davis – became Bowie's most enduring and was retained for the following five albums. The next of these was *Station to Station*. Like many Bowie albums, *Station to Station* is an album of contrasts. *Hunky Dory*, as mentioned, is often regarded as a album but could equally be viewed as proto-glam. Likewise, *Young Americans*, which conventional wisdom holds is a funk album, contains songs of a far more poppy nature – we need look no further than the title track. The *Station to Station* album is often regarded as wildly experimental. Such readings are possibly based largely on the title track, which consists of at least three contrasting sections. The song might legitimately be called a 'piece' and commences with a long grinding opening which gathers pace and builds anticipation – an opening gambit that would not wash with today's Spotify generation for whom the introduction of a song must grab immediately, lest the listener moves swiftly on, never to return. It continues with a middle movement of driving and emphatic rhythm-driven force before concluding with soaring melodies and an insistent groove. Elsewhere the album contains the more conventional funk rhythms of 'Golden Years' and the lilting groove of 'TVC 15'.

These exceptions notwithstanding, the overall theme of the album is bleak and desolate. Until now, the focus in Bowie's songs had always been outward looking. His attention was on expanding his view of the world – indeed, his universe – and exploring all of its possibilities. Carlos Alomar's influence from 1974 onwards can be seen clearly when looking back to consider the situation before his arrival. On the *Ziggy Stardust* album, released in 1972, Bowie wrote about space exploration, alien visitors, utopian futures, stardom, moonage daydreams. By no means was the focus entirely on positive imagery – he dipped into future dystopias, notably in 'Five Years', and yet even then he focused on what he saw around him, chronicling the reactions of everyday people to the impending disaster.

Over subsequent years and successive original albums, Bowie's focus began to shift. While the focus remained outward-looking, on 1973's *Aladdin Sane* the emphasis was on schism and fracture – a theme that was perfectly illustrated by the lightning bolt that splits Bowie's face in Duffy's cover image. Bowie famously described *Aladdin Sane* as 'Ziggy in America' and the album has a distinctly American vibe. Indeed an American location, representing the geographical location that inspired it or which was the site of its initial creation, was appended to the titles of all but two of the tracks on the first UK release of the album. The trend is broken only by 'Lady Grinning Soul' (London) and the older rerecorded 'The Prettiest Star' (Gloucester Road); otherwise New York (twice), Seattle-Phoenix, Detroit, Los Angeles and New Orleans are name-checked on the record label, along with RHMS *Ellinis*, the ocean liner which transported Bowie home in late 1972. Throughout is the vibe of trashy bar and decadence, nowhere more than on

'Lady Grinning Soul' and 'Aladdin Sane'. Elsewhere, in 'Panic in Detroit' we see urban breakdown and guerrilla warfare with drug references and allusions to escape and seclusion whereas 'Drive-In Saturday' imagines a future in which people have forgotten how to reproduce and watch old movies in order to relearn.

So, overall, *Aladdin Sane* is an album of Bowie considering the world as it is being revealed to him and conjecturing about where current paths might lead. The theme is extended still further with *Diamond Dogs*, Bowie's next album of new material, the lyrics of which are preoccupied with urban decay, addiction and death, opening with the spoken 'Future Legend' which describes a post-apocalyptic world in which "the last few corpses lay rotting on the slimy thoroughfare," and moving through 'We are the Dead', which makes reference to 'dancing where the dogs decay, defecating ecstasy'. The protagonist of the title track warns that:

> I'm sure you're not protected, for it's plain to see
> The Diamond Dogs are poachers and they hide behind trees
> Hunt you to the ground they will, mannequins with kill appeal.

Again, the outlook may be bleak, but the focus is entirely on the world as Bowie finds it and the likely consequences of continuing on the present path. This began to change after 1975's funk/soul album *Young Americans*. At this time, it was standard practice for artists to be contracted to produce an album or more per year, sometimes more. By 1976's *Station to Station*, the gaze is altogether more inward-looking. Bowie's state of mind and the results of his drug intake are there for all the world to see in 1974 when he is interviewed by Dick Cavett, and his insularity is written all over his next few albums. Consider 'Station to Station': "Here am I, tall in my room overlooking the ocean,"; 'What in the Word' from *Low*: "So deep in your room, you never leave your room / Something deep inside of me – yearning deep inside of me"; and 'Sound and Vision' also from *Low*: "Pale blinds drawn all day / Nothing to do, nothing to say."

The antithesis of his usual arch-assembler approach, this insular way of working grew from Bowie's own situation. The stories of him living entirely on peppers and milk, while exaggerated, illustrate the unhealthy mindset and lifestyle that Bowie had adopted at the time. He talked about having moved to Los Angeles precisely because he hated it there and was intrigued to see what would happen to his writing in such an environment. What happened was that he produced one of the standout albums of the decade. He also became very noticeably ill and, having always been thin, lost so much weight as to seem almost skeletal. Photos of him at the 17th Annual Grammy Awards in 1975 show him with alarmingly sunken cheeks and teeth which seem to protrude from his diminished features. The lyrics in the album show a focus on the work of British occultist Aleister Crowley, as had been the case with 1971's *Hunky Dory*.

Bowie slept on the couches of friends at times, including that of Deep Purple's Glenn Hughes. And on one occasion asked Hughes to have sex with his wife, Angie. Hughes obliged. Bowie also began to flirt with Nazi imagery and described Adolf Hitler as, "one of the first rock stars", a statement which he unsurprisingly came to regret and retract, explaining that he was "out of [his] mind, totally. Completely crazed." At Victoria Station in May 1976, Bowie was photographed apparently giving a Nazi salute. Footage of the incident shows that in fact he was caught by the camera in mid-wave to gathered fans, but the fact that such an incident seemed credible illustrates the situation in which Bowie found himself. His latest character, the Thin White Duke, who is reported in the 'Station to Station' track as "throwing darts in lovers' eyes" perfectly personified the stark dangerous nature of the paths he pursued at this time.

In the midst of all the madness, a voice of reason and a bastion of sanity was Carlos Alomar. Although by no means immune from the excesses of the period, Carlos was also a settled, married man. When Bowie was unwell, it was Carlos and his wife, singer Robin Clark, who fed him.

In the annals of music history, there are tales of collaboration and symbiosis that transcend mere partnership. One such story is that of David Bowie and Carlos Alomar, a guitarist whose impact on Bowie's life and career cannot be overstated. Their union not only produced some of Bowie's most iconic works but also played a pivotal role in salvaging Bowie's life and career during a tumultuous period. Even the most resilient artists face moments of vulnerability. For Bowie, the late 1970s marked such a period. Plagued by personal demons and struggling with substance abuse, Bowie found himself teetering on the brink of self-destruction. It was at this critical juncture that Carlos Alomar entered his life.

Carlos brought not only his musical prowess but also his unwavering support and friendship to Bowie's tumultuous world. Their collaboration began in the mid-1970s and would endure for decades. And it was during Bowie's darkest hours that Alomar's influence proved to be truly transformative. While Bowie was grappling with addiction and a creative slump and his personal life was in disarray, Carlos Alomar arrived in his life – and his steadying presence and musical ingenuity breathed new life into Bowie's career. Alomar's contributions as a guitarist infused Bowie's music with a fresh vitality, revitalising his sound and reigniting his creative spark.

But Carlos's impact extended far beyond the realm of music. As Bowie battled his inner demons, Alomar provided unwavering support and guidance, serving as a confidant and friend during Bowie's darkest hours. It was Alomar who stood by Bowie's side, offering a beacon of hope in times of despair and reminding him of his inherent worth as an artist and human being. Together, Bowie and Alomar embarked on a journey of redemption and reinvention. Their collaboration yielded some of Bowie's most seminal works, including the critically acclaimed albums *"Heroes"*, *Lodger* and *Scary Monsters (And Super Creeps)*. These albums not only showcased Bowie's musical evolution but also served as a testament to the transformative power of creative partnership.

Entwined with his personal steadying influence is his funk/soul chops – bringing to Bowie the thing that helped him survive the end of glam rock in 1974. A change of direction just in time. Bowie had surrounded himself with people with fresh ideas that he could assemble and reorder into something new and unique, and Carlos Alomar was at the forefront. Just as it is likely that Bowie's story would have unfolded differently if John Cambridge hadn't recruited Mick Ronson, so it could have been entirely different – both personally and professionally – if Bowie hadn't happened upon Carlos Alomar at the very time that he needed him.

Chapter 4
A NEW CAREER IN A NEW TOWN

The fact that Bowie's teaming up with Carlos Alomar also coincided with his reunion with Tony Visconti meant that another solid team was in the process of forming. Tony's influence on *Young Americans* stands as a testament to the impact a producer can have on shaping the sonic landscape of a record. At the same time, Carlos's influence meant that the album marked a significant departure from Bowie's previous work as he delved into soul, funk and R & B influences. The album remains a landmark in the careers of all three.

Although Visconti's relationship with Bowie dated back to the late 1960s, it was with *Young Americans* and alongside Carlos Alomar for the first time, that Visconti's influence would, to date, be most keenly felt. Perhaps his greatest contribution to *Young Americans* lay in his ability to capture Bowie's vision while simultaneously pushing the boundaries of his sound. Together, they set out to create an album that would bridge the gap between the rock and soul genres, drawing inspiration from the rich musical tapestry of 1970s America.

Visconti's technical expertise played a crucial role in

shaping the album's distinctive sound. In contrast to the do-it-yourself punk-style ethic that Bowie brought as producer to *Diamond Dogs*, Visconti brought a meticulous attention to detail to the recording process, working closely with Bowie to craft the album's lush arrangements and dynamic production that would have been lacking if Bowie had replicated his *Diamond Dogs* approach. He made full use of the studio to layer different instruments and vocal tracks to create a rich, textured sound.

One of the most notable aspects of *Young Americans* was the use of rhythm and groove. Drawing on his knowledge of jazz and funk, Visconti helped Bowie infuse the album with a sense of rhythmic vitality that set it apart from his earlier work. 'Fame' and 'Young Americans' crackled with energy, driven by infectious basslines and propulsive drumming that owed as much to the dance floors as they did to the rock clubs of London.

Visconti's influence on the album extended beyond the realm of production. As a trusted collaborator and confidante, he provided valuable feedback and guidance to Bowie throughout the creative process. Tony has reported that Bowie often felt somewhat intimidated by his producers. Perhaps the greatest advantage of working with Tony was that Bowie was working with a friend. Tony's keen ear and musical intuition helped Bowie refine his songwriting and arrangement skills, enabling him to fully realise his artistic vision.

His role as a mentor and collaborator allowed Bowie to tap into new sources of inspiration and creativity. Together, they explored a wide range of musical styles and genres, drawing on everything from classic soul and funk to avant-garde experimentation. This spirit of eclecticism and innovation would become a hallmark of Bowie's later work, as he continued to push the boundaries of popular music.

Perhaps most importantly, Visconti's influence on *Young Americans* helped pave the way for Bowie's subsequent reinventions and transformations. By embracing new sounds and styles, Bowie demonstrated a willingness to take creative risks and push the boundaries of his artistry – a trait that would define his career for decades to come.

Come November, Visconti, Bowie and the band returned to the studio – Sigma Sound in Philadelphia – to complete the album that they had had to interrupt in August due to the tour. Memorably, when recording at Philly was complete, David invited a group of fans to who had been waiting outside the studio for weeks, to listen to the album. It was a nice gesture to reward the fans for their dedication and also reflected Bowie's eagerness to know what his fans would think of this album that was a great departure from previous offerings. Patti Brett, one of the 'Sigma Kids', reports that they listened to the album quietly and then, when it was finished, someone shouted: "Play it again!" and everyone got up and danced – a ringing endorsement.

With principal recording done, Tony and David repaired to the Record Plant in New York to do further work on the album with Harry Maslin as engineer, and it was during this time that David bumped into John Lennon at a club and arranged a meeting in Bowie's hotel. A nervous Bowie asked Tony to be present to "buffer" things. This was during the period of Lennon's "Lost Weekend" during which he was separated from Yoko Ono and in a relationship with May Pang, who attended on this occasion (and later became Tony Visconti's wife). David's nervousness manifested itself as a quiet withdrawnness, during which

Tony and John discussed recording and music. Tony mentioned that he'd worked with Paul McCartney but hadn't received a credit and John said that he'd been planning to call Paul but now wouldn't bother as Tony had reminded him "what a fucking cunt he is". For his part, David spent most of the evening sketching until John asked him for some paper from the pad and the two challenged each other to draw caricatures of each other.

Bowie had liked the sound of Visconti's London studio so much that he suggested that Tony should return to London to mix the album. Tony was more than happy to return home and see Mary and their son, Morgan, where, guided by 18 pages of notes and suggestions from Bowie, he duly mixed the album and added strings to three tracks. He shared the results with David but was dismayed at what happened next. Bowie relayed that he had recorded a version of Lennon's 'Across the Universe' and John had added some acoustic guitar. Furthermore, they had recorded another song – a future hit called 'Fame'.

To say that Tony was disappointed to have missed out on the chance to collaborate with John Lennon would be to understate the matter somewhat. "David," he said, "I would have gladly paid to travel on Concorde to be at that session," he said. Concorde could have transported Tony from London to New York City in less than three hours. Bowie did apologise: not only had he worked with Lennon in Tony's absence but he had also recorded two songs for the album Tony was producing without Tony, with Harry Maslin as producer instead. 'Fame' was Bowie's first number one hit in America. In his autobiography, Tony jokingly but ruefully reflected that this must be his payback for declining to produce 'Space Oddity'.

After the pair had worked closely on the mixing of *Diamond Dogs* and as co-producers of *Young Americans*, the partnership seemed to be looking strong again. Perhaps the later *Young Americans* sessions with Harry Maslin influenced the decision, but it was Maslin, not Visconti, who Bowie turned to make his next album, the mighty *Station to Station*. However, when Bowie produced Iggy Pop's *The Idiot*, he again turned to Tony to help with the mixing. Their working relationship was at last cemented. Without the arranging prowess and ideas of Mick Ronson for Bowie to assimilate, Bowie could have been left somewhat forlorn had he not reunited with Tony and combined and repurposed his ideas with his own.

* * *

Bowie's next album, which was to be called *Low*, is regarded by many as his greatest achievement, although there are of course other contenders for the title. The album was recorded in September and October of 1976, and Bowie by now was profoundly fed up with the idea of rock 'n' roll and of being a rock star. Drugs and the rock lifestyle had brought him to the brink of madness and David realised that it was time to take another path. As he later said, if he'd continued, he would not have survived the '70s. Told that rock 'n' roll had been good to him, he retorted, not unreasonably, "Well, I've been good for rock 'n' roll."

For *Low*, many musicians returned, including the now rightly celebrated D.A.M. Trio rhythm section – Dennis Davis, Carlos Alomar and George Murray. The highly influential new boy was Brian Eno, Bowie's collaborator for the next three albums and later during his creative renaissance in the 1990s. Eno had been a member of Roxy

Music during their early most experimental stage and he and Bowie had crossed paths when Roxy supported Bowie in 1972. No longer with Roxy, Eno was by then producing left field, experimental ambient albums which had caught the attention of Bowie at the right time as he turned away from rock music.

David made a call to Tony Visconti, with Brian Eno listening on an extension. He explained that the pair had been exploring ideas, combining Brian's ambient music with David's style and that it was going really well. His question for Tony was: "What can you bring to the table?" Tony explained that about a new piece of equipment that he had acquired, the Eventide Harmonizer.

"What does that do?" David wanted to know.

Tony's answer sealed the deal. "It fucks with the fabric of time!"

The answer assured all three men that they were on the same track. To hear what fucking with the fabric of time sounds like, just listen to the drums at the beginning of 'Sound and Vision'. It's hard to imagine the album without this sonic input and it could have been so different had Bowie not been prepared to assimilate and repurpose Tony's input – and if Tony had not been prepared to give it.

When I asked Tony about the Eventide Harmonizer a few years ago, he told me, "It was impossible to change pitch without changing the speed when all we had to work with was analogue tape. So, really, the Eventide Harmonizer really did fuck with the fabric of time!"

It was the Harmonizer which was used to drop the pitch on the snare drum which made the sound of *Low* so distinctive and groundbreaking. The album that is often regarded as a creative high point for Bowie was in fact the one which he struggled most for inspiration – certainly lyrically. 'Sound and Vision' deals with this directly, describing its narrator as patiently waiting for inspiration to strike: "I will sit right down / waiting for the gift of sound and vision" while his frustration is shown in lines like, "Pale blinds drawn all day / Nothing to do. Nothing to say."

Of the eleven tracks, six were entirely or mainly instrumental. That it is now widely regarded as among his most influential works is down to a number of factors. His characteristic ability to alter course at the right moment – largely turning away from popular music at the perfect time to both bemuse and intrigue his audience – was a huge factor, but the wildly creative approach of Eno was another. Eno used a set of cards called Oblique Strategies to send the sessions in unpredictable directions. Thus, the musicians, were instructed via the cards: "Don't be afraid of cliché", "Make an exhaustive list of the possibilities and do the last on the list" or "Look closely at the most embossing details and amplify them." Given Eno's strategies, Visconti's use of the studio, Bowie's new approach to songwriting and the influence of European sounds such as Krautrock, it is little wonder that the album sounded completely different from anything else that had been in the public consciousness to date.

The album was not entirely inaccessible to a mainstream audience, however. Far from it. It also contained accessible pop songs. 'Sound and Vision' made number three in the UK and the album number two, while in the United States, it made a healthy number 11. Rather than touring with the album, Bowie, almost perversely, chose instead to tour as part of Iggy Pop's band, playing keyboards almost anonymously as a band member, ostensibly equal to the other players. A little over 10 years later, he would do something similar by forming the band Tin Machine and taking the role of equal band member – to whatever extent that is possible when one member of the band is a superstar.

The team of Bowie, Eno and Visconti continued throughout the rest of the '70s, producing albums that owed much to Eno's ambient style, particularly with the first two albums and also a number of bona fide classic hit singles including 'Boys Keep Swinging' and '"Heroes"' which – incredibly in retrospect – reached only number 24 in the UK charts and has only latterly undergone a critical reappraisal, becoming a ubiquitous anthem for sports teams and for those who triumph over adversity.

Over the course of three albums, Eno manifested himself as one of Bowie's most significant and influential collaborators – perhaps the person from whom he collected more than any other. For his own part, Bowie's life was at a crossroads – perhaps a number of crossroads if the metaphor will stretch that far. During his time in LA he had become increasingly paranoid, eating too little but ingesting too much. In 1975, in the still recent wake of the split with the Spiders, he had also split with his manager and the architect of his success, Tony Defries, which had left him feeling bruised. To add to his woes, his relationship with wife Angie was falling apart. He was becoming more drug dependent and putting less and less effort into his relationships, isolating himself in fits of paranoia while Angie's volatility was such that according to Bowie, living with her was "like living with a blowtorch". Thus, the studio became the place where he was free to use his imagination and influences to create his own domain away from the pressures of the outside world, and where Eno and Visconti were the perfect partners with whom to fashion the audio landscape. Bowie brought the rock pedigree and songwriting prowess, Eno the avant-garde experimentation and Visconti the studio know-how and technological expertise.

Eno took the role of disruptor as much as creator – sometimes contributing ideas but often skewing those of others into something previously not considered. Whereas until now, Bowie's lyrics had tended towards storytelling, he began to abandon narrative and embrace abstraction under Eno's influence, in rather the same way that Monet and Renoir abandoned the accuracy and precision of realism and embraced the short, broken brush strokes and immediacy of impressionism – often creating their works on the spot or *en plein air* rather than planning the details in advance. Eno's Oblique Strategies cards had been developed by him the previous year alongside artist Peter Schmidt. In addition to other messages, they contained instructions or observations such as "Don't be afraid of things because they're easy to do", "The tape is now the music" or "Do the washing-up"! If a creative impasse was reached, the cards were produced and the command followed. It seemed a natural evolution from a technique Bowie had used to good effect in the past.

Bowie had long used the "cut ups" technique that he borrowed from William Burroughs to produce novel perspectives in his lyrics. In 1980, he explained the technique to Andy Peebles:

> *You're thinking, oh, let's go back to the Wall. The Wall keeps cropping up. So, you got the Berlin Wall and you've got different episodes happening outside of it. You're getting somebody trying to jump over the Wall. Then you write*

> *paragraphs. Well, this is what I do, anyway. This is only one example. I'd write a paragraph from the jumper's point of view. I'd write a paragraph from an observer's point of view on this side of the Wall and then an observer's point of view on that side of the Wall, so you've got three different points of view. And then I cut them up and I reshuffle them and I pull them out in three- or four-word phrases and put the parts together. And then from that, I can either take exactly what is laid out and utilise that as a new theme; you get some quite original little things coming out of it... a fourth point of view, in fact, that one hadn't thought about before or, I can take it exactly as it reads, or I will then re-sort it out. There are no rules, there are no ground rules. I mean there is no, "This is what it is, you are not allowed to deviate from that." There's no rule system in it. It's a tool of writing; a way of writing to promote a new perspective on something that might have got stodgy. I don't use it all the time these days. I used to use it far more.*

A representation of the Bowie working method is shown in Alan Yentob's film from the *Diamond Dogs* era which shows various typewritten lines being cut, moved and re-combined to form known Bowie lyrics. The method is now so well-known and connected with Bowie that in 2022, when Bowie's organisation set up twin shops in London and New York to celebrate his 75th birthday, they included a tower adorned with cut-up Bowie lyrics for fans to arrange and combine, with interesting – and, of course, often rude – results.

Eno's strategies built on this as well as taking some of the creative pressure away from Bowie himself. Eno also gave Bowie permission to break boundaries. When Bowie had completed a fragment of a song, 'Breaking Glass', which he intended to build into a completed track, Eno encouraged him to leave it as a fragment. "Don't normalise it," he urged, and therefore the song, in its studio form, remains a 1 minute, 51 second fragment whose brevity, as well as its lyrical and sonic strangeness, stands as its greatest asset.

Bowie continued with his "cut ups" technique for years, although to a lesser degree. By 1980, his methods had evolved somewhat. In the 'David Bowie is' exhibition, which opened in London in 2013, two pieces of graph paper were exhibited which illustrate this. These are also available for all on the excellent website *Pushing Ahead of the Dame*, authored by Chris . Here we can see that Bowie's method no longer involves physical cut ups – if indeed it ever did – and he now jots down various lines and thoughts before selecting and building. Here we see him gathering ideas, thoughts and fragmentary lines which would later be assembled into lyrics, particularly 'It's No Game' and 'Up the Hill Backwards'. Also present is the line, 'The vacuum created by the arrival of freedom. And the possibilities it seems to offer. If one can grasp them' which Nicholas Pegg discovered was purloined from Hans Richter's *Art and Anti Art*.

If the timing were different, it would be tempting to read a Spinal Tap-ism into the lyrics. In the illustrious mockumentary *This is Spinal Tap*, bass player Derek Smalls explains what it is like to be in a band with great creators, Nigel Tufnel and David St. Hubbins, "two totally distinct types of visionaries. It's like fire and ice and I feel my role in the band is to be kind of the middle of that, kind of like lukewarm water." *Half of me freezing, half of me boiling, I'm nowhere in between*, Bowie wrote on his sketch sheet. Sadly, the film did not appear until four years after *Scary Monsters*, which must surely be a lesson to all of us who try to produce readings of the words of others – though it's also worth remembering Bowie's own words, echoing the thoughts of the French literary theorist Roland Barthes, that once he has completed his recording and released it, it is "interpreted, and correctly interpreted" by anyone who listens.

* * *

Bowie had been living in Los Angeles – a place that he claimed to hate and was therefore good for his writing. It was not good for his health, however. It is clear that he wasn't eating well or sleeping properly and was taking too many drugs. Photos from the Grammy Awards ceremony in 1975 show a skeletal-looking figure and things had hardly improved. Bowie later said, "I'm quite certain I wouldn't have survived the '70s if I'd carried on doing what I was doing."

Thankfully, Bowie had enough perception and resolve to realise and act. In the summer of 1976, just before starting to work with Eno and along with a similarly afflicted Iggy Pop, he moved to Berlin, where he hoped the lifestyle would suit him better. Many years later, he remarked on the irony of the fact that he had unwittingly moved to the "smack capital of the world" – a world which is depicted quite starkly in the film *Christiane F.,* in which the eponymous character, a teenager addicted to heroin, is a devoted fan of Bowie, who appears in concert. However, Bowie and Pop, having changed their backdrop in an effort to get clean, did not partake and were on the road to better health.

It is too often assumed by the uninitiated that Brian Eno produced the three albums on which he appears, the so-called Berlin Trilogy – *Low*, *"Heroes"* and *Lodger*. Certainly, Bowie, true to form and nature, osmosed the ambient sensibility from him and, as ever, made it his own. However, it was of course Visconti who produced all three; Eno is listed among the musicians. On *Low* he is listed as having contributed vocals, Splinter Minimoog synthesizer, Report ARP synthesizer, Rimmer EMI, EMS Synthi AKS synthesizer, piano, Chamberlin keyboard and guitar treatments. The fact that each individual type of synth he played is listed perhaps emphasises his contribution, which was undoubtedly great, or it may reflect the fact that the synth was a novel instrument and the types of instrument quite distinct, but it does seem strange when viewed from a distance of nearly five decades. After all, the different types of guitar played by Carlos Alomar are not listed.

Tony Visconti is often forced to correct the record on this. Very recently (as I write) he had this to say on Facebook:

> *I just listened to an uninformed #NPR announcer reviewing a new Brian Eno documentary that's just been released. The Heroes album and single were produced by David Bowie and myself, no other producer is credited as you can see on the official album credits below. They 'reported' that Eno produced Heroes (he was the co-writer and played some synth parts). I know some of you will find this funny, that I have to STICK UP FOR MYSELF when this gaff is made again and again. I'm sure some of you will post the "hilarious" animation that portrays me as goofy. Eno is a fabulous, innovative musician and composer and I have great respect for him. Make no mistake about that.*

To which, Bowie added in 2000, "Over the years not enough credit has gone to Tony Visconti on those particular albums. The actual sound and texture, the feel of everything from the drums to the way that my voice is recorded, is Tony Visconti."

Released in January 1977, *Low* marked a significant departure from Bowie's previous work and was instrumental in shaping the sound of the late 1970s while also drawing influence from the Krautrock movement.

Visconti's involvement in the album was instrumental, not only in its production but also in its conceptualisation and execution.

Low was, of course, the first of Bowie's so-called Berlin Trilogy, a series of albums that were heavily influenced by the ambient and electronic music of the time, particularly from artists like Kraftwerk and Brian Eno. The album emerged during a period of personal and artistic transformation for Bowie, and Berlin, with its rich cultural history and burgeoning music scene, would provide a perfect backdrop for Bowie's reinvention – though the description *Trilogy* is something of a misnomer. *Low* was largely recorded near Paris at the famed Château d'Hérouville, which had been the studio in which *Pin Ups* had been recorded in 1973 and which Bowie as producer had used for the Iggy Pop album, *The Idiot*.

Tony Visconti's production on *Low* was characterised by a willingness to experiment and push boundaries. One of the most notable aspects of his work on the album was his use of innovative studio techniques, particularly in the treatment of sound and the creation of new textures, evident in the way the album was structured and embraced wholeheartedly by a receptive Bowie: the first side featured more conventional rock and pop songs, while the second side delved into more experimental, instrumental tracks.

Indeed, the album's original title was *New Music: Night and Day,* a title designed to emphasise the contrast between the two styles of music.

The use of the Eventide Harmonizer, which he famously used on the drums, creating a distinctive, otherworldly sound that became a defining feature of the album was particularly evident in tracks like 'Sound and Vision' and 'Breaking Glass', in which the drums have a uniquely fractured, echoing quality that adds to the album's avant-garde feel.

Of course, it was by no means a done deal that Tony would produce *Low*. The last Bowie album he had fully produced was 1970's *The Man Who Fell to Earth*. Since then, he had been credited on *Diamond Dogs* with mixing and strings on '1984', and had produced *Young Americans* (except for the tracks that that Harry Maslin produced after Tony had left town to mix the tracks) but he had not been involved in *Station to Station* at all.

By the summer of 1976, Tony was in need of a *change*. Married to Welsh singer Mary Hopkin, he felt she was using their young family as an excuse not to work in an industry that can be tough on young artists. Tony's record label, Good Earth, was not doing as well as he had hoped, and he had not produced a T. Rex album since 1974's poorly received funk excursion *Zinc Alloy and the Hidden Riders of Tomorrow*, which earned Marc Bolan no credit for its exploration of funk 18 months ahead of *Young Americans* but criticism for supposedly ripping off the title of *The Rise and Fall of Ziggy Stardust and the Spiders from Mars*.

It was therefore a good time for the producer to receive a call from David Bowie's Switzerland home.

The collaboration between Tony Visconti and Brian

Eno was, of course, a significant factor in the creation of *Low*. Whereas Eno's influence brought a new dimension to Bowie's music, incorporating ambient sounds and experimental structures, Visconti's role in this collaboration was crucial; he acted as a mediator and translator of Bowie's and Eno's ideas into tangible musical forms. Visconti's ability to blend Eno's abstract, ambient concepts with Bowie's more structured songwriting resulted in a unique and cohesive sound. The instrumental tracks on the second side of *Low*, such as 'Warszawa' and 'Art Decade,' are prime examples. Visconti's production ensured that these tracks were not just atmospheric interludes but integral parts of the album's narrative, reflecting Bowie's internal and external landscapes – in the same way that the separation of the album into, broadly, a side of songs and a side of instrumentals does.

Arch collector of ideas and talent that he was, David used the skills of engineer Eduard Meyer in the studio, too:

> *When I warmed up a little bit first with Tony Visconti and later with David and when they realized that I was a studied cellist, they asked me if I would like to record a cello track on the recorded title 'Art Decade' on side 2 of* Low. *I agreed and Tony and I sat together and wrote a score for me, as I am a score musician. So I sat down in the 'Big Hall by the Wall' and recorded my track and they liked it and asked for another one. I played a low and a high version and finally we got eight cello tracks. Tony mixed them into the big sound of Brian Eno's synthesizers and when you listen to the song, you can hear the scratching of the bow on the strings, a sound that could not be reproduced by an electronic instrument.*

The production of *Low* under Tony's guidance had a deep impact on the music industry. The album's innovative use of technology and unconventional structures influenced a wide range of artists and genres, from post-punk to new wave and beyond. Visconti's techniques, particularly the use of the Harmonizer, were ahead of their time and contributed to a new understanding of what was possible in music production.

The album marked another turning point in Bowie's career, helping him transition from the glam rock icon of the early 1970s, through the funk of *Young Americans* and the stark soundscapes of *Station to Station* into a pioneer of avant-garde music. It was now that people started referring to Bowie as the chameleon of rock. He had changed direction before, but it took two or three about-turns to develop a reputation. For his part, Bowie rejected the label, pointing out that chameleons change to blend with their environment whereas he liked to stand apart from his.

However, Visconti's ability to facilitate this transformation was crucial, showcasing his versatility and deep understanding of the artist's vision while the album's critical and commercial success cemented Visconti's reputation as one of the most innovative and influential producers of his era.

By now, Bowie and Visconti seemed like an unbreakable partnership and there was no question of anyone else producing the next album, *"Heroes"* – the only album of the Berlin Trilogy to be recorded mainly in Berlin, specifically at Hansa, a studio in West Berlin close to the Wall. The image of fracture and division suited Bowie's work well: there are many themes that pervade Bowie's work throughout the decades, and alienation, duality and splintering are among the most prevalent. To work in the most divided city of all seemed almost normal and expected and, 500 yards from the Wall, armed guards kept watch, adding to the atmosphere of menace. On board, as with *Low*, were the D.A.M Trio rhythm section – Dennis Davis, Carlos Alomar and George Murray – along with virtuoso guitarist Robert Fripp, from King Crimson, vocalist Antonia Maass and Eno, of course, on synthesizers, keyboards and guitar treatments as well as playing his customary role of bringing controlled randomness and disorder to proceedings. Towards the end of the recording of *Low*, Bowie and Visconti had decamped to Hansa Studio 2 to complete recording and had mixed the album at Hansa by the Wall. For *"Heroes"* they settled in the same studio as Bowie moved from his hotel suite to an apartment and prepared to settle, for a time, in a city which offered him anonymity. Whereas *Low* was recorded in an extemporaneous manner, for *"Heroes"* there was now an established template, laid during the sessions for the previous album, for them to follow.

Low had been short on lyrics and partially instrumental both for artistic reasons and because David struggled for inspiration. Indeed, the lyrically sparse 'Sound and Vision' deals with the subject of the profound writer's block that Bowie was experiencing. *"Heroes"* would follow the same pattern.

It's hard to fathom now that 'Heroes' was barely noticed when it was released as a single. This despite a concerted effort to promote both the single and album – in stark contrast to his efforts to promote *Low* which were practically non-existent. Bowie even recorded French and German language versions of the song.

Bowie's sponge-like ability to soak up the details of his environment and deliver it back as art was never more evident than on this song, hit or not, which is set in the space between worlds. The narrative concerns two lovers, one from each side of the Wall, meeting and stealing a moment together, and encapsulates the idea of love and humanity overcoming insurmountable odds. For my money, the genius of the song lies in its presentation of the stolen moment lasting simultaneously "just for one day" and "forever and ever". The notion of, as William Blake would have it, holding eternity in the palm of one's hand. The idea of the battle or struggle against time is accentuated with the line, "we can beat them".

For decades, David told the story of seeing two young lovers meet daily by the Wall and imagined a story in which the pair were from opposite sides of divided Berlin, meeting to steal a little time. Co-producer Tony Visconti later revealed that the image of the two lovers was suggested by a clandestine meeting between him and backing singer Antonia Maass. David needed to finish some lyrics, so Tony took a walk one afternoon along with Maass. According to Tony, the pair were having a "dalliance" and shared a kiss near the Wall, seen by David from the window of the studio, an incident which prompted David to imagine the scenario he used for the song. Knowing that Tony was married to singer Mary Hopkin, Bowie did not share the details of the identities for the "two young lovers" when he told the story.

On this, Chris O'Leary reports that Antonia Maass was later interviewed by Tobias Ruther and said that she and Tony could not have been the subject of or inspiration for the song because the lyrics for '"Heroes"' had been completed before their affair began. Another friend, artist Clare Shenstone, had supported David after the loss of his father and, during the making of *'"Heroes"'*, he called her to visit him. David explained that she had appeared in his dreams and she said that she had dreamed of swimming with dolphins – a reference that made it into the final lyrics. In the book *Album to Album*, Paolo Hewitt says that the influence for these images is two works or art: a painting called *Lovers Between Garden Walls* by Otto Mueller which shows a young couple meeting in the space between two tall stone walls, and a short story by Alberto Denti di Pirajno, *A Grave for Dolphins*.

Of course, it is not for me to suggest which among these stories is truer than another. What is true is that the juxtaposition of this intimate, human connection against the stark, oppressive symbol of the Cold War encapsulated the themes of love, defiance and hope amidst adversity. The Wall, a representation of division and conflict, contrasted sharply with the simple yet profound act of love, inspiring Bowie to weave this imagery into the fabric of the song.

The anonymity of Berlin suiting him better than star-obsessed Los Angeles, Bowie was doing better by now both physically and mentally and in 1977 he reports, "I'm happy now. Content. I feel more than a product on an assembly line and no more a means of support for 10,000 persons who seem to revolve around every fart that I make," an assertion which not only attests to the relative serenity he now felt but also to the resentment he had and continued to feel about the position of responsibility he unwittingly found himself in. As Bowie remarked in 2001, Berlin, a city in which the inhabitants were uninterested in the presence of a pop star, was a great place to be anonymous and therefore a good place to both lose oneself and find oneself. Visconti reports a joyous time recording the album. Again, the fact that Bowie had a strong and stable band gave him the platform he needed to reach higher.

Each member of the band knew they had set a high bar when making *Low* and were determined to reach even higher for the new album. They knew each other well by now and were in confident mood. The efficiency with which the studio was run naturally helped the smooth running of the sessions, allowing the artists and players to focus on creation and performance. Eduard Meyer was the house engineer and his casual effectiveness created a stable environment. Tony, as we have seen, always knew that a solid band was needed for Bowie to grow. It seemed that he was also now benefiting from a wider steadiness provided by production personnel, the studio itself and the city.

Whereas previously sessions might go on into the night and start up very late the next day, now, according to Meyer:

> *He was a steady worker… He booked his sessions going along with the daily opening hours of Hansa Studio. Normally the evening and the night was reserved for his private enterprise. But depending on free studio time he sometimes worked from evening into the night, but never longer than eight hours. Sometimes he enjoyed the nightlife of Berlin and was happy to have enough sleep afterwards.*

With the highly competent and motivated backing band of the D.A.M. Trio, the backing tracks were "a dream" to record in Tony's words. He was clearly enjoying himself as he describes them as being "over too quickly".

Once the highly efficient rhythm section had completed their work, it was time to call in a lead guitarist to add flair and originality. Robert Fripp was known as the guitarist and leader of King Crimson, the highly influential experimental progressive rock band. For the *"Heroes"* recordings, the use of an amplifier for Robert Fripp's guitar was felt to be superfluous. Instead, Fripp fed his guitar through an array of pedals. Eno then used his "magic briefcase" of envelope filters and synthesizers. Three takes were recorded this way in what Tony describes as a two-man performance. When the takes were combined, the effect was the mesmerising, constantly mutating sound that is the introduction to '"Heroes"'. As a collector of ideas and influences, Bowie was always happy to allow his musicians the space to create. Why hire highly creative people unless you're prepared to give them the space to create.

In just two days, Robert had completed his lead guitar parts and just Tony and David remained in the studio, at which point not a single vocal had been recorded and not a single lyric or melody written. Bowie would arrive at the studio with a few lines of lyrics, which would be committed to tape. Recording would then stop while Bowie scribbled out a few more lines, sometimes singing them to himself to try out various options before having Tony drop the next few lines into the song. The process was surprisingly fast, usually taking around two hours from scratch to completed multitracked vocal recording.

A tour followed the release of *"Heroes"*. Tours rarely had official names in those day, and this one is variously known as the Isolar II Tour, The Stage Tour or the Low/Heroes Tour. The tour's stage design was minimal, dominated by stark, industrial lighting that reflected the cold, mechanical feel of the Berlin albums. Bowie's setlist included tracks from *Low* and *"Heroes"*, as well as reinterpreted versions of earlier hits like 'Fame' and "Rebel Rebel."

Isolar II was notable for its departure from flamboyant

costumes and theatrics, focusing instead on music and Bowie's brooding, detached persona on stage. Later performances were captured in the live album *Stage*. The tour helped cement Bowie's legacy as a constantly evolving artist, pushing the boundaries of rock music.

The familiar team of Tony Visconti, Brian Eno and the D.A.M. Trio convened during a break in the Isolar II tour in September 1978.

Necessarily, the live tour band became the studio band.

Adrian Belew had taken the place occupied by Robert Fripp on the last album. In true magpie style, Bowie had come across Belew when the latter was playing guitar in Frank Zappa's band and was impressed by his unique, experimental style. Brian Eno had seen Zappa in concert and recommended that David catch a show – which he did, along with Iggy Pop, in Berlin. During a part of the show when the band left the stage for Zappa to perform a solo, Belew walked to the rear stage area and found Bowie and Iggy by the mixing board. Belew told Bowie he'd like to work with him, and the immediate response was: "Great. How would you like to be in my band?" Although Belew countered that he was already a member of the band currently performing on the stage, Bowie said that his tour was due to start two weeks after Zappa's concluded and suggested they have dinner together.

They initially had a clandestine meeting in a limo outside Belew's hotel. "It was like something out of a spy film," Belew remarked, before heading to Bowie's favourite restaurant to continue the conversation. Incredibly, of the thousands of restaurants in Berlin, Bowie's favourite also appeared to be Zappa's. He and the band were enjoying a meal at the same place. "Quite a guitar player you have here," Bowie ventured.

"Fuck you, Captain Tom," said Zappa, clearly unimpressed with the obvious subterfuge and demoting Bowie to a rank lower than his 'Space Oddity' character. Bowie tried to make conversation, but Zappa repeated his previous words.

"So you really have nothing to say?" said Bowie.

"Fuck you, Captain Tom," said Zappa, one final time.

Bowie, Belew and Bowie's assistant Coco Schwab simply left. "I thought that went rather nicely," Bowie concluded. It was clear that Belew could not continue with Zappa's band, and he joined Bowie for the tour and album. Bowie knew that it was good to surround himself with talented people whose ideas could combine and create. Throughout his career he employed wildly creative guitarists whose job it was to sprinkle magic over a solid basis laid down by the rhythm section. He found the ideal replacement for Fripp in Belew.

Sean Mayes, the pianist on the tour and album, remembered arriving at Mountain Studios, right on the lake, and walking up a winding staircase to an intimate recording facility and finding Tony Visconti sitting at the mixing desk, "cheerful and relaxed as usual – he always creates an easy atmosphere in the studio, helping to relieve the tensions which can arise". Mayes further reported that the rough backing tracks had been completed before his arrival and all had provisional names, such as 'This Tangled Web' and 'Portrait of the Artist', none of which survived the process as, true to past performance, Bowie had not written any lyrics as yet. They would be written during the second set of *Lodger* sessions in New York at the end of the year, following the Far East leg of the tour.

Lodger is one of a few of Bowies albums with no title track, a distinction it shares with *Hunky Dory*, *Low* and two later albums, *Earthling* and *Hours* (we should also perhaps mention *Pin Ups* and the two albums called *David Bowie*), and it is uncertain where the title came from. We do know that working titles for the piece included *Despite Straight Lines* and *Planned Accidents*, the former emphasising the intended deviant nature of the recording and the latter the methodology that Bowie, Eno and Visconti had in mind – that they would set up situations in which mistakes were likely to occur and then use them as if they had been intended. Bowie later remarked that a mistake repeated becomes a new arrangement.

On one song, 'Boys Keep Swinging', the band swapped instruments – an idea followed earlier by Bowie as producer of 'Fall in Love with Me' on Iggy's *Lust for Life*. Guitarist Carlos Alomar switched to drums, Dennis Davis from drums to bass and George Murray swapped his bass for keyboards. In the event, not all planned accidents produce outcomes that are acceptable on pop albums. Carlos's drums were retained but Dennis Davis's bass was rerecorded by Tony and pushed to the fore in the mix to form a counter-melody whereas the keyboard stylings of George Murray were apparently not used –, only Bowie and Eno are credited with playing the instrument on the song. It is worth noting, though, that Sean Mayes remembers it differently: Tony was on bass, he says, George on drums, Carlos on organ ("I think") and Brian on piano.

Perhaps the most famous – and contentious – example of Eno's efforts to shake things occurred when he selected his eight favourite chords – and for anyone who's wondering, according to Sean Mayes, those chords were B flat, F,

C, E, G, E flat, A minor and C minor. Eno then instructed the band to find a groove and play whichever chord he pointed to. This "back to school" approach did not sit well with the seasoned professional musicians. Simon House, the violin player, recounts that it "sounded terrible" whereas Carlos felt that the experiment was "stupid" and "bullshit". Visconti agreed that it was not the greatest idea to tell three guys who came from the roughest part of New York and Bowie himself conceded that these "'art prank' ideas didn't go down too well," despite his encouragement.

Another planned accident involved guitarist Adrian Belew who, like Fripp before him, had arrived at the session later than the rhythm section and, along with Mayes and House, was adding lead parts and detail to the tracks. To his surprise, he was asked to sit in a small room away from everyone else and was then fed a song through his headphones without ever having heard it. This was another "art prank", of course, designed to elicit unexpected results. He could see no one and was told that he would hear a click track and he was then to start playing. "Play what?" he asked.

"Whatever you think of."

"What key?" But it was made clear that he would have no more information. Belew was allowed two or perhaps three goes at each song and, as soon as it was felt he was becoming wise to the key and structure of the song, they would stop and move on to the next one. The blistering solo at the end of 'Boys Keep Swinging' was constructed from takes built in this way. "It was supposed to be called *Planned Accidents,* so I was the accident," he said in 2023.

The song itself, as ever with Bowie, can be interpreted in any number of ways. Commentators have read it as, for example, a young man's ode to the possibilities ahead, a bisexual man's imaginings of a gay man envisaging a straight life, a gender blurring return to the preoccupations of the early '70s. Certainly, lines like "other boys check you out", "you'll get your share", "life is a pop of the cherry" and "you can wear a uniform" seem to point towards teenage fantasies, whereas the very title, including the word *swinging*, seems to either reference the 1970s preoccupation with wife-swapping or fluid sexuality.

The video for the song and television appearances around the time confirm that Bowie was returning to question gender roles. Directed by David Mallet, the video captures Bowie's flair for performance and his subversive approach to gender norms, creating a visual experience that is as thought-provoking as it is entertaining.

The video opens with a simple but striking scene: Bowie, dressed in a suit, stands against a background reminiscent of '70s pop shows – latex tubes and a staircase, a minimalist setting drawing attention to Bowie himself, emphasising his performance and the song's lyrics.

As the song progresses, Bowie is joined momentarily by multiple versions of himself dressed in drag and singing backing vocals. Their appearances are fleeting but serve to disrupt the image of Bowie, who hams it up while singing the song complete with exaggerated Elvis/rock star moves.

The first character appears as a sophisticated woman in a long dress, moving gracefully and exuding elegance yet chewing gum while the second moves slowly wearing a tight dress and heavy make-up, her mannerisms exaggerated for effect. The third character is a glamorous and confident older woman, her outfit and demeanour suggesting a sense of empowerment and self-assurance. The first two tear their wigs off and smear their make-up in an apparent rebellion against the trappings of the construct of femininity while the elderly woman simply approaches the camera and blows a kiss.

This was the first time since 1974 that Bowie challenged traditional gender norms. By performing in drag, Bowie blurred the lines between male and female, emphasising the performative nature of gender itself.

Bowie also appeared on *Saturday Night Live* on which he performed three songs, 'The Man Who Sold the World', 'TVC 15' and 'Boys Keep Swinging'. For 'TVC 15' he performed in a dress. The other notable performance was on the *Kenny Everett Video Show*, a performance that was also directed by David Mallet and filmed back-to-back with the video. It features Bowie in a black jumpsuit delivering another straightforward performance against a similar backdrop as is used for the official video and dropping to his knees to play the violin during the solo outro. Kenny Everett then appears in the guise of his character 'Angry of Mayfair' and proceeds to chase David around the set – Everett's character appears as a city gent in pinstripes and bowler hat from the front but viewed from behind is seen, in true Kenny style, to be wearing stockings suspenders and a bra. Bowie hams it up beautifully, showing comedic chops every bit the match of Everett's.

It must surely be no coincidence that all three performances toy playfully with gender roles. In his early career, Bowie was unsure of himself as a performer and therefore adopted characters and played roles in order to make the task of performing easier. He became dangerously immersed in his characters, to the extent that he was unable to shake them off and was at great risk of becoming a casualty. By this point, he had managed to leave the characters behind and gained the confidence to perform as himself without the need for guise or disguise, and he now appeared to have sufficient distance from the characters to be able to adopt a role once again, but this time as a plaything rather than an identity. David remained in control, and neither Ziggy or the Thin White Duke took over.

On *Lodger*, he revisited his past in other ways, too, collecting influences from his own past as well as from people and environs. The music for 'Move On' is the Bowie-penned Mott the Hoople classic 'All the Young Dudes' played backwards. It is also often said that 'Fantastic Voyage' and 'Boys Keep Swinging' have exactly the same chords. As a bedroom standard guitarist, I can see a couple variations but it's very close.

Lodger sees Bowie at a creative peak, and yet the album splits opinion and received mixed reviews at the time. Some feel the slow ending of the Eno relationship is showing – certainly there was a certain amount of unspoken strain in the studio, although both were far too polite to vocalise it. Also, the studio used for mixing was not of the standard usually used by David and Tony, which many feel produced a muddy-sounding mix. When I interviewed Tony in 2017, he said:

> *David and I always agreed that Lodger could've been mixed better. We were doomed to mix it in a dreary New York studio due to a deadline. We should've rented outside equipment, but companies that do that didn't exist at the time. We always said that we would remix it someday and that's what I would like very much to do. It might happen!*

Indeed, he was already working on a new mix for *Lodger* for the box set *A New Career in a New Town*. When released, it was far crisper than the original and many lost details could be heard.

Whilst this book is mainly focused on the way Bowie collected musical influences, he also gathered from other areas of the arts, so before we leave *Lodger*, it is worth considering its sleeve. For the first time since *Aladdin Sane*, Brian Duffy, known in his professional capacity simply as Duffy, was invited to take the photos for the new album. *Aladdin Sane* must surely rank as Bowie's most iconic cover with its breathless, stark but fresh image of an other-worldly looking Bowie with lightning bolt fractured face. It must surely be his most famous cover and one of the most celebrated record sleeves of all time. This sleeve was to be very different. Inspired at least partly by the self-portraits of Egon Schiele – particularly *Self-Portrait as St. Sebastian*, it has been suggested – Bowie wished to appear "unsightly, dishevelled and broken", as Kevin Cann puts it in the *Five Sessions* book that he co-authored with Chris Duffy. This was the very antithesis of the *Aladdin Sane* image. In a 1977 interview, Bowie had been asked about being a 'hero'. The atmosphere in the interview is strange, alternating between levity and tension. "People make you a hero," the interviewer opines.

"No, they don't," says Bowie.

"For them."

"No, they don't. You don't make me a hero. I know I'm not a hero."

He goes on to explain that he has cast off the characters and that the interviewer is talking to David Bowie the person, not a character. Later in a 1999 interview with Jeremy

Ziggy Stardust – 1972 Photo Duffy © Duffy Archive

Les Rendez-Vous du Dimanche interview for French Télévision, Paris – October 1977 © Philippe Auliac

Paris, June 1977 for the premiere of *The Man Who Fell to Earth* movie at Gaumont Cinema © Philippe Auliac

Scary Monsters – Album Cover Image – 1980
Photo Duffy © Duffy Archive

Paris Orly Airport départage to Madrid during the promo 1987 Showcase
© Philippe Auliac

Plaza Athénée private session in Paris – May 1977 © Philippe Auliac

Lodger Album Cover Polaroid – 1979 Photo Duffy © Duffy Archive

Plaza Athénée private session in Paris – May 1977 © Philippe Auliac

London Astoria Show – December 2, 1999 © Philippe Auliac

Backstage in Paris with Tin Machine – 1991 © Philippe Auliac

Paris Roissy Airport coming from Amsterdam – October 1977 © Philippe Auliac

Paris, June 1977 for the premiere of *The Man Who Fell to Earth* movie at Gaumont Cinema. With his assistant Barbara Dewitt © Philippe Auliac

London Victoria Station – May 2, 1976 © Philippe Auliac

Wembley Empire Pool during Suffragette City – May 3, 1976 © Philippe Auliac

Ziggy Stardust,
Santa Monica Civic Auditorium – October, 1972 © Boris Yaro

Close-Up at Milano Alcatraz – December 4, 1999 © Philippe Auliac

Reality Tour at the Lille Zenith – November 2003
© Philippe Auliac

The Raw Moon on stage at Wembley Empire Pool – May 5, 1976
© Philippe Auliac

Rehearsal at London Riverside for Reality TV Broadcast show
© Philippe Auliac

Last show of Station to Station tour in Paris during Jean Genie –
May 18, 1976 © Philippe Auliac

The Famous Smile during the Cigale Tin Machine Show, Paris – 1989 © Philippe Auliac

Station to Station tour in Paris during Word on a Wing – May 17, 1976 © Philippe Auliac

Paris – July 3, 1987
© David Currie

Les Arenes de Nimes,
14 July 2002
© Philippe Auliac

Artwork by Helen Green for
David Bowie Glamour fanzine

Paxman he agrees that "David Bowie" is a character in itself, but nevertheless, we start to see a little more of the man behind the performance.

It is perhaps no surprise, then, that for the cover of *Lodger* he wished to appear as the direct opposite of the Aladdin Sane/Ziggy Stardust characters of yore.

Bowie, wearing a conventional suit with shirt to reveal his midriff and tie askew, was attached to a stand in a horizontal position. Incongruously clutching a comb in his bandaged right hand, he has a fishing line tied across his nose to suggest injury or disfigurement. Behind is a backdrop of a domestic bathroom. To get a good vantage point for the shots, Duffy climbed into the rafters of his studio and shot from there. The result was a series of striking, mundane yet unsettling images which would be sure to undermine and confound the expectations of both audience and critics.

This was not subversive enough for Bowie, however. He elected to discard the beautifully shot high resolution image and use a Polaroid test shot for the cover. Furthermore, he decided that, as the album was to have a gatefold sleeve, he would place his legs on the front and his face on the rear of the gatefold. David was, as ever, confounding expectation, in keeping with the themes of the album itself. This lo-fi subversive approach may well have been influenced by the punk movement, too, with its do-it-yourself methods and cut up, fragmentary styles.

As the next album to consider is 1980's *Scary Monsters*, this might be a good place to consider the sleeve of that record, which was also photographed by Duffy. Not long after the *Lodger* session, Duffy gave up his studio, disillusioned and fed up with having to do commercial work for demanding clients. However, he was happy to oblige when Bowie asked him to shoot the cover for his new album, and made use of the studio owned by his son, Chris.

For the *Scary Monsters* shoot, David asked costume designer Natasha Korniloff to create "the most beautiful clown in the circus." The intricately designed and beautifully crafted Pierrot costume exceeded expectations and Natasha herself was present on the day to arrange the costume and ensure everything was perfect.

Make-up artist Richard Sharah, introduced to David by Steve Strange, was responsible for David's make-up. David admired Steve's make-up and the vibe of the Blitz Club in Soho, leading to Steve and some of the Blitz kids being featured in the 'Ashes to Ashes' video, walking along the beach.

Later, Chris Duffy shot photos of David for the press, by which time his make-up was smudged, so Chris photographed him smoking, with his costume half removed – a clown returning to reality after the circus was over. For the fanzine, Chris wrote, "My photos show a softer more vulnerable look. I was very happy with the outcome. It's rather special to me now, as it's the only time my father and I worked together, both as professional photographers shooting the same subject." The smudged make-up echoed the 'Boys Keep Swinging' video and would be used again in the videos for 'China Girl' in 1983 and 'Jump They Say' in 1993.

When it came to designing the cover, Bowie picked artist Edward Bell who drew a beautiful picture of David in the clown make-up. He then placed it over a torn image of Duffy's photo so that the Bell image was visible and only the shadow from Duffy's image remained. The cover is now very well-known, even iconic. There was no suggestion that

Duffy was unhappy with the *Lodger* cover, but when it came to this, he was not pleased. Edward Bell takes up the story:

> *David … came down with Duffy to my basement flat in Earls Court where I lived and worked – and there was the picture. Bowie just took one look at it and said, "I love it." Duffy didn't say a word, he was absolutely furious – though I didn't know there was anything wrong at the time.*
>
> *And then, a couple of months later I got a phone call from Duffy who said, "I think you're the nastiest opportunist shit I've ever met…" I hadn't realised how cross he would be. I just thought, Well, I've been asked to do a job, that's the way I see it – Duffy sees it differently, but that's the way I've been asked to do the job.*

It had been Duffy who had introduced Edward Bell to Bowie and now he felt usurped. "Over the years," Chris says, "there has been some controversy about the mix of Edward Bell's input into the *Scary Monsters* album and the friction between the two creatives. However, ultimately yet again, a fantastic album cover came together." Which seems a good place to let things rest.

For the next album, it was felt that the partnership with Eno had run its course and, after three albums, a return to more of a rock-oriented approach would be a good thing. The spirit of experimentation did not leave along with Eno, but there was a step change. "He actually sat down and wrote the songs for a change," said Tony Visconti. Like previous outings, the backing tracks were laid down early, sans melody or lyrics. However, rather than write lyrics on the spot, Bowie elected to take a couple of months away from the studio to write, resulting in songs that seemed more finely crafted and less fragmentary than on previous outings. Not all influences are artistic ones, of course, and Paolo Hewitt notes that the business situation with Bowie's former manager, Tony Defries, was also a factor. This was not the first time that business had affected artistic decisions.

A few years ago, I interviewed Tony Zanetta who revealed that *Pin Ups*, Bowie's 1973 covers album, was made partly because David's songwriting publishing deal was coming to an end. If he had recorded new material, it would have been covered by his previous, less lucrative, contract, but by putting out an album of other people's songs, he was able to save his own music for the new deal. In the mid-'70s, Bowie found himself free from the management of Defries but subject to a severance deal which gave Defries a very sizable portion of Bowie's earnings – 50 per cent by many accounts – until 1982. This being the case, Bowie had been content to produce albums which satisfied artistically but fared only moderately well commercially. It's worth reflecting that the albums that build Bowie's reputation as an arch avant-garde experimenter may have been influenced by this financial situation.

Despite the arrangement still being in effect, when David arrived at The Power Station to record the next album in early 1980, he told Tony Visconti that this would be the first conscious attempt to make a record with commercial appeal since *Young Americans*. Interestingly, he told Andy Peebles later that year almost the opposite:

> *I think I gave up the idea of markets way back when the whole process of business and selling records for records' sake and ... when it became a question of what kind of content do you give an album so it gets higher sales? When that sort*

of great puzzle came up, I thought, "Well, that's defeating the whole point of why I'm writing." It just doesn't make any sense. And I wasn't enjoying it. That was round about Aladdin Sane period, just before The Spiders's break-up. And that was one of the few albums where I put content in to try and accumulate record sales, which was a gross mistake all the way round. It's just something I didn't want to do. And I've found out since, of course. Then I got quite into the idea of, "Well, they just have to take me for what I am," sort of thing, and I stuck with that.

The LP sounds new and fresh even though the album uses lots of old ideas. 'Ashes to Ashes' is based on the story of Major Tom. The music for 'Scream Like a Baby' is taken from 'I am a Laser', written by Bowie for the band the Astronettes, a vocal trio he had been mentoring in 1973–74 which included his then girlfriend/muse Ava Cherry. 'People from Bad Homes', another Astronettes song written by Bowie, turned up as a lyric in 'Fashion', a song which borrowed its opening chords from 1976's 'Golden Years'. 'It's No Game' was based on an old song called 'Tired of my Life', which he is reported to have written aged 16. Bowie the Collector had never been more to the fore than on this album.

By 1980, he had amassed enough of a back catalogue to begin to borrow from himself. 'Ashes to Ashes' revisits and expands the narrative of Major Tom, the character first introduced in Bowie's 1969 hit 'Space Oddity,' adding a layer of depth and complexity to Bowie's musical lore, reflecting both artistic evolution and personal introspection.

In 'Space Oddity,' Major Tom is an astronaut who becomes stranded in space, a character symbolising isolation and the unknown. The song, released during the height of the space race, captured the imagination of a generation fascinated by space exploration. Major Tom's fate is left ambiguous, a haunting ending to a poignant tale.

Over a decade later, 'Ashes to Ashes' provides a stark and more sombre update on Major Tom's story. The song reveals that Major Tom has become a 'junkie', a possible metaphor for Bowie's own struggles with drug addiction during the 1970s. The lyrics – "We know Major Tom's a junkie / Strung out in heaven's high / Hitting an all-time low" – convey a sense of disillusionment and despair. This reimagining transforms Major Tom from a tragic hero to a cautionary figure, reflecting Bowie's personal battles and societal changes.

In the Andy Peebles interview, Bowie expands on how he approached the revisiting of Major Tom's story:

> *So, when I was thinking of how I was going to place Major Tom in this. Hence, 10 years later on, what would be the complete disillusion with the great dream that was being propounded when they shot him into space 10 years ago and had such wonderful ideas. … But now we come to him 10 years later, and we find that the whole thing has soured because there was no reason for putting him up there. So, the most disastrous thing I could think of is that he finds solace only in some kind of heroin-type drug… actually being that the cosmic space itself is feeding him with an addiction, and he wants now to return to the womb from whence he came.*

The idea of returning to the womb is borrowed, like much of Major Tom's story (and the title of 'Space Oddity' of course) from the film and novel *2001: A Space Odyssey* in which astronaut David Bowman undergoes a similar transformation. As ever, Bowie produces a new piece of art based upon the stimulus.

Musically, 'Ashes to Ashes' combines Visconti's production techniques with a haunting melody, and nursery rhyme-style chants, juxtaposed against the complex emotional landscape of the lyrics.

The song's eerie synths and layered vocals create an atmosphere of alienation, further emphasising Major Tom's descent. By revisiting Major Tom in 'Ashes to Ashes,' Bowie not only continued a much-loved narrative but also used it as a vehicle for self-reflection and critique. This evolution of Major Tom's story showcases Bowie's ability in blending personal experiences with his art.

Tony Visconti summed up the song perfectly: 'Ashes to Ashes' ... took everyone by surprise, because what was expected was another of those bizarre kind of things off *Low* or "*Heroes*" or *Lodger*, and here's this most conventional pop song ever written, with a cute verse, a cute chorus, and then the devastating stab where he tells the world that Major Tom's a junkie, and kills off the character he created and glorified all those years before. That was the beauty of that track, because he'd been sardonically looking for some way to get rid of Major Tom once and for all."

A major contributory factor to the success of 'Ashes to Ashes' was that groundbreaking video. It features surreal and striking imagery, including Bowie in a Pierrot costume, which became one of his most memorable visual personas: ask anyone about the video and they'll describe Bowie walking along a beach in a clown suit. Key though that image is, it would have been exhausting if the full 3 minutes, 33 seconds was nothing but that. Director David Mallet included three other key scenes which set the tone as much as the clown. Bowie is shown in a padded cell, at times sitting in a chair singing, at others cowering in a spot-lit corner. He is also shown sitting in a chair in a kitchen in which appliances are exploding but a woman continues working undeterred; in another scene, he is strapped to a wall wearing a grotesque padded suit into which pipes are inserted, presumably pumping his body with liquid. As Nicholas Pegg points out, "clown, spaceman and asylum inmate are staples of his former work, again fuelling the notion that 'Ashes to Ashes' is a comprehensive exorcism of the past". For the beach scene, an innovative tool called Paintbox was used to colour the sky and sea black. For extras in the beach scenes (and briefly in the kitchen) Bowie chose Steve Strange and three other attendees of the Blitz club, the famous London club run by Strange and frequented by Boy George, Spandau Ballet, Marilyn and Rusty Egan, who were soon to find fame themselves.

Strange, who gained notoriety for his club by refusing entry to Mick Jagger, spearheaded the New Romantic movement and would shortly be having hits with his band Visage. His club ran famous Bowie Nights. I talked at length to Steve Norman of Spandau Ballet about this and he described how the movement came off the back of punk with its "no future" messaging and nihilistic live-for-the-day ethos. By the early '80s, the future that the punks had promised would never come had arrived and they had to figure out what to do with it. And if you lived in a grotty part of town, better to stand out and be fabulous than to blend in.

Famously, Steve Strange and the others, led by Bowie, walk along the beach pursued by a large digger. At intervals,

Strange and the others raise an arm and drop towards the ground – a manoeuvre that was precipitated by Strange's fear that his long robes would be caught in the wheels of the oncoming farm machinery. Bowie liked the look of it and incorporated it into the video.

Filming wasn't entirely smooth and at one point proceedings were interrupted by a man walking his dog. The story is relayed in Dylan Jones *David Bowie: A Life*:

> *Mallet asked him if he wouldn't mind moving, and pointed out Bowie sitting outside the catering van. "Do you know who this is?" he asked. Sharp as a tack, the old man responded with, "Of course I do. It's some cunt in a clown suit." Sometime later, Bowie remembered, "That was a huge moment for me. It put me back in my place and made me realise, 'Yes, I'm just a cunt in a clown suit.'"*

Clearly, Bowie already had it in mind to shake off his past, taking Major Tom and the trappings of the video out for one last spin around the block, but if he needed any reinforcement that he was doing the right thing, this must have been it.

Scary Monsters...and Super Creeps marked a pivotal moment in Bowie's career, blending artistic innovation with commercial success. Following the experimental Berlin Trilogy, *Scary Monsters* was both a return to more accessible rock music and a continuation of Bowie's and Visconti's fearless exploration of new sounds and themes. Its success can be attributed to a combination of its critical acclaim, chart performance, influential singles, and enduring legacy.

Scary Monsters was met with widespread critical acclaim upon its release. Critics praised Bowie's ability to merge the avant-garde with mainstream appeal. The album was seen as a culmination of his artistic journey in the 1970s, synthesizing the experimental elements of his earlier work with a newfound clarity and focus. 'Ashes to Ashes' and 'Fashion' were highlighted for their innovative production and lyrical depth, cementing Bowie's reputation as a visionary artist.

Commercially, *Scary Monsters* was a significant success. The album reached number one on the UK Albums Chart and performed well internationally, breaking into the top 20 in the United States. This commercial success was bolstered by the strong performance of its singles, which received substantial radio airplay and charted highly. 'Ashes to Ashes' became one of Bowie's most iconic songs, reaching number one on the UK Singles Chart. Its success was mirrored by 'Fashion' and the album's title track, both of which also performed well on the charts.

The legacy of *Scary Monsters* extends beyond its initial commercial and critical success. The album is often regarded as one of Bowie's best, frequently appearing in lists of the greatest albums of all time. It marked the end of an era for Bowie, serving as a bridge between his 1970s work and the subsequent changes in his musical direction during the 1980s. The album's themes of identity, fame and personal reflection resonate with listeners and continue to be relevant.

Scary Monsters also influenced a wide range of artists across different genres. Its fusion of post-punk, new wave and art rock elements inspired many musicians in the 1980s and beyond. Artists such as Trent Reznor of Nine Inch Nails and bands like Radiohead have cited Bowie and this particular album as a significant influence on their work. By seamlessly blending avant-garde experimentation with mainstream appeal, Bowie created a work that not only defined his career but also left an indelible mark on the music industry.

In a 2020 interview, Carlos Alomar described the album as "one of my favourite albums. There are no soul songs on that album, man. But what a great album. But I have no idea why we didn't tour it. We did the songs live eventually of course. I love it.

If indeed he did see the album as a means to shake off his past selves, it is perhaps no surprise that Bowie didn't want to prolong matters by touring. His record deal was coming to an end, his deal to share his earnings with Tony Defries was ending soon and his divorce from Angie was finalised. His addiction problems were behind him. Little wonder he was looking to the future. First, though, he must disappear for a while.

Chapter 5
MODERN LOVE

Perhaps Bowie's masterstroke was to lie low for a few years, musically. This was not a tactic that had been employed by pop and rock musicians hitherto, although it became *de rigueur* later for artists to become elusive. In Bowie's case, it probably wasn't done as a tactic so much as for pragmatic reasons. Bowie certainly had reason to wait. With this RCA contract ending and his arrangement with Defries expiring at the end of September 1982, he gave himself something of a break from music. Not a complete break. He recorded a number of one-off records, notably, the wildly successful 'Under Pressure' with Queen which became a massive hit in the UK in 1981 and broke the top thirty in the US singles chart – a territory in which he had had little success since 'Fame' and 'Golden Years' in the mid-seventies. For the erotic horror film *Cat People*, he wrote and recorded 'Cat People (Putting Out Fire)' with Giorgio Moroder. RCA released the compilation *ChangesTwoBowie* and a single from it, 'Wild is the Wind', for which Bowie made a performance video. At the end of '82, RCA released the Bing Crosby duet, 'Peace on Earth / Little Drummer Boy' lifted from a 1977 TV Christmas special. RCA also released, in beautiful packaging, a set of Bowie singles, called *Fashions*.

Bowie was not musically idle by any means, but no new album and therefore no new grand musical statement was forthcoming.

Another incident that prompted Bowie to keep away from the public gaze happened around this time. While performing in *The Elephant Man*, Bowie was interviewed by Andy Peebles of Radio One. Bowie discussed the play at length, went through the details of many of the tracks from *Scary Monsters* and reflected on his career to date, touching on his time working with John Lennon on the *Young Americans* album five years earlier. Just the night before speaking to Bowie, Peebles had also conducted a three-hour interview with Lennon and Yoko Ono. Then, just the day after Peebles spoke to Bowie, Lennon was shot by Mark Chapman.

At the performance of *The Elephant Man* the following evening, there were two empty seats in the front row, reserved for John and Yoko. Further down the same row, another unoccupied seat had been reserved by Chapman. "I can't tell you how difficult that was to go on," David said. Later it was discovered that Chapman had circled Bowie's name in his copy of the programme for the play. His girlfriend reported that, if Chapman had not killed Lennon, the next on his list was Bowie.

It is no surprise that David wished to keep out of the way for a while.

In the meantime, Bowie focused on his acting career. He appeared as himself in *Christiane F.*, recorded the opening for *The Snowman*, starred in the niche Brecht play, *Baal*, for the BBC, and released a soundtrack EP. He took leading roles in the vampire story *The Hunger*, and the acclaimed

Merry Christmas, Mr. Lawrence, the latter of which, at least, was praised by critics.

As an artist of great standing – and bankability – there was of course a number of potential suitors queuing up to woo Bowie. Geffen, Columbia and EMI-America were keen. RCA were also eager to regain his signature. EMI won the day, for a five-album deal reported variously to have been worth between $10 million and $20 million. Bowie's recording session with Queen may well have helped sway things in EMI's direction as Freddie Mercury had waxed lyrical about the trust and freedom his band was afforded by the record company.

Bowie was to emerge from his self-imposed exile in spectacular fashion. But first he needed to make an album. And, newly free of previous ties and monetary obligations, he wanted it to be a hit. For this, he turned to producer Nile Rodgers — a partnership that may have seemed an unlikely one, but of course, knowing Bowie as the arch assembler as we do, we shouldn't be surprised

By the early 1980s, David Bowie was already a big star, if not quite yet the global superstar he was about to become, known for his genre-defying music and innovative approach to art and fashion. He had conquered the 1970s with a series of groundbreaking albums, from the glam rock of *Ziggy Stardust* to the experimental sounds of *Low* and *"Heroes"*. However, by 1982, he was at a crossroads in his career and was seeking a new direction that could re-establish his place in the rapidly changing music scene of the early 1980s.

Nile Rodgers, on the other hand, was a celebrated musician and producer who had co-founded the disco band Chic and produced hits for artists like Diana Ross and Sister

Sledge. Chic's music was characterised by its sophisticated arrangements, infectious grooves, and a distinct blend of funk, disco and soul. Rodgers' career was also in a state of flux; the disco era had waned a little, and he was eager to branch out and prove his versatility as a producer.

The first meeting of the pair was an inauspicious occasion, to say the least. Nile Rodgers walked into a bar with his "hanging buddy" Billy Idol, who had moved from the UK to America to launch his solo career. In the bar was David Bowie, but dressed in a debonair suit, he went unrecognised by the pair for at least 20 minutes. Eventually, Idol twigged and uttered the immortal line, "Bloody Hell, it's David fucking Bowie!" and, simultaneous with the word *Bowie* vomited onto his clothes and the floor. Without missing a beat, Billy used his sleeve to wipe the vomit from his mouth and extended the same hand to Bowie with a friendly "Hello, mate!" while an amused but embarrassed Rodgers beseeched Idol to back off a little. Many people would have made their excuses and disappeared but to Bowie's lasting credit, he remained and had a long conversation with Rodgers, impressing him with his deep knowledge of jazz and other music. They also found they had mutual friends in Carlos Alomar, Robin Clark and Luther Vandross.

When Bowie asked Rodgers to produce his next album, the producer assumed he would be making a typical art rock-style, groundbreaking Bowie album. Puzzled, he asked why the singer had chosen him, and was told, "Because you make hits!" This was a Bowie in his mid-thirties ready to capitalise on the hard work that he had put into his career. Rodgers told *Musician* magazine in 1983, "David could have gone with any producer – white or black – he wanted. He could have gone with Quincy Jones and a more sure-fire chance at a hit. But he called me up. For that, I felt honoured."

It was decided that the first move would be to decamp to Montreux to record demos of the songs that were slated for the album. They were joined by Turkish multi-instrumentalist Erdal Kızılçay, and Bowie shared his songs using a 12-string guitar. After this, and armed with demos that could be used to share the basic ideas with the rest of the band, they moved to The Power Station in New York – a familiar location for Bowie – to record the album. The band consisted of a combination of top session musicians and others who were known to Rodgers. Bernard Edwards and Tony Thompson, the other members of Chic, were brought in towards the end of the sessions and used sparingly. Rodgers explains that, through drug use, they had become less punctual and reliable, and he didn't want that to cause problems with Bowie – especially as they were working a pretty regular 10.30 a.m. – 6.30 p.m. schedule. When Bernard did come in to contribute his bass on 'Without You' he nailed it in one take, much to Nile Rodgers's relief. Carlos Alomar had also been slated to work on the album, but Bowie's new management offered him the minimum union rate, whereas Carlos had been used to receiving a modest raise with each new album and hadn't worked for the minimum payment for many years. Some have seen this as a way to make sure Carlos did not appear on the album without the need to actually tell him so.

Texas guitarist Stevie Ray Vaughan was also present. He and Bowie had crossed paths the previous year at a festival in Montreux and chatted and got along, but even so Vaughan was very surprised to get a call from Bowie to ask him to work on the album but Bowie was collecting a team of disparate talents in the hope of fusing their influences to produce a fresh sound and perspective.

Four weeks had been booked in the studio in December 1982 and recording was concluded in just 17 working days. Even allowing for subsequent mixing, this was one of the quickest albums to record in Bowie's career, a major reason being that Bowie, who had not yet signed his record deal with EMI America, financed the recording himself. For the first time ever, Bowie didn't play a note of music on *Let's Dance*, justifying this in an interview by saying, "This is a singer's album!" Rodgers recalled Bowie sitting on a sofa "while I made his album". The parallels with Tony Visconti's experience 13 years earlier on *The Man Who Sold the World* are apparent. Tony himself had been slated to work on the album and had been asked to keep the month of December free to start pre-production work. During the time that Bowie was in the studio in Montreux cutting the demos, Tony called Bowie's assistant, Corinne "Coco" Schwab, to talk about travel arrangements. "Well," he was told, "you might as well know. David's in the studio with someone else. It's working out well, so he won't be needing you. He's very sorry." With that, their decade long partnership ended for the time being.

With the album done, Rodgers had indeed turned Bowie's folky 12-string pieces into triumphant dance hits. He explained that if a song is called 'Let's Dance', you'd better make sure you can dance to it!

For many, this was a new, smooth Bowie with all the jagged edges removed, dressed, as he was on the subsequent tour, in pastel suits with bouffant hair and a bow tie hanging untied around his neck. Contemporary reviews were mainly positive, though some sounded notes of caution. Charles Shaar Murray said, "It's warm, strong, inspiring and useful. *Let's Dance* is irresistible." The *Guardian* said it was:

> *Highly impressive, yet mildly disappointing. This is partly because he is now working within an instantly recognisable, accessible field, as opposed to experimenting with Fripp or Eno, and partly because his brilliant single, Let's Dance/ Cat People, contributes the best two tracks on the album.*

Rolling Stone said that "*Let's Dance* sounds great; it's all beat, brains and breathiness. The album's most intelligent strategy is its utter simplicity," but that, "for all its surface beauty, though, there's something thin and niggling about *Let's Dance.*"

Michael Watts had this to say: "His new album seems to be a step sideways. He's not doing anything particularly new and I suspect for the first time ever his fans are up there with him and he's not ahead of the game."

Bowie's commercial breakthrough was not regarded as his masterpiece, even as he rose to the greatest fame of his career and even as he reaped the financial rewards that had eluded him for so long.

The album itself certainly does feel a little thin. After three years away, his new offering proffered only eight tracks. Furthermore, one was a cover (Metro's 'Criminal World'), one was a reworking of a song he had written and recorded with Iggy Pop long ago ('China Girl') and one was another reworking of an earlier song, 1982's 'Cat People (Putting out Fire)', leaving just five new Bowie-penned recordings. Perhaps it is little wonder that the album was completed in 17 days.

Nevertheless, the album was a huge commercial success, going on to sell well over 10 million copies and sealing Bowie's place in the rock super league. As for Nile Rodgers, he would say for decades to come that it altered the trajectory of his life, establishing him as a record producer as well as a writer and musician.

* * *

With the album complete, Bowie travelled the following month to Australia to make the videos for 'Let's Dance' and 'China Girl' with David Mallet. Although never one to appropriate cultural influences lightly, the representation of traditional Australian culture is striking and is another example of Bowie seeking inspiration from beyond his usual sphere. The video is a vibrant and visually arresting piece that complements the song's upbeat, danceable rhythm while delivering a powerful social message. The video intertwines themes of cultural identity, economic disparity and the impact of Western culture on Indigenous peoples.

The video begins with scenes of a young Aboriginal couple in the Australian Outback, juxtaposed with images of urban life. As the video progresses, the couple is seen trying on Western clothing and dancing in a bar, highlighting the encroachment of modern culture on traditional ways of life. The pair eventually returns to the outback, barefoot, dancing on the red earth – a potent symbol of reconnection with their roots.

The visual storytelling in 'Let's Dance' is both celebratory and critical. On one level, it captures the joyous, communal spirit of dancing, with people of different backgrounds coming together. On another level, it serves as a critique of cultural assimilation and the loss of Indigenous identity in the face of globalisation.

The iconic image of red shoes, referenced in the lyrics and shown in the video, becomes a metaphor for this cultural conflict. While the shoes initially symbolise the allure of Western modernity, their eventual abandonment reflects a rejection of this imposed identity.

Bowie's decision to use his platform to highlight these issues was significant, especially in the context of 1980s' pop music, which often shied away from such themes. The 'Let's Dance' video is not just a promotional tool for the song but a bold statement on cultural resilience and the complexities of identity in a globalised world, making it one of Bowie's most memorable and impactful music videos.

On the back of this success, it was time for Bowie to take the show on the road. The tour was named Serious Moonlight after the line in the 'Let's Dance' song. In a video interview included in the VHS video of the tour, Bowie explains, "It's an Americanism I just like. Serious this. Serious that. So, I called it [adopts cheesy American accent] 'Serious Moonlight Tour'. It had no real meaning behind it." He goes on to explain that he didn't want to do a serious show because these usually "get analysed to death. And I don't always agree with what is said …"

The success of *Let's Dance* was immediate and overwhelming. The album became one of Bowie's bestselling records, reaching number one in the UK and several other countries. The Serious Moonlight Tour would be vastly different in tone and scale from anything he had undertaken before, reflecting Bowie's new position as a mainstream superstar.

The tour was a defining moment in the career of Bowie, marking his transition from avant-garde artist to global pop icon. This was his first concert series since 1978, and represented a seismic shift in his artistic direction. Where previous tours had been characterised by theatricality, experimentation and complex narratives, the Serious Moonlight Tour was a straightforward celebration of Bowie's newfound mainstream success. The stated aim was to remind people that the songs they'd heard on the radio for years were by Bowie. The tour not only solidified his status as one of the most influential figures in popular music but also set a new standard for live performances in the 1980s.

The Serious Moonlight Tour officially began on 18 May 1983, in Brussels, Belgium. From the outset, it was clear that this tour was designed to be a spectacle. Bowie was known for his theatricality and knew that, on this scale, he must deliver. Bowie and his team invested heavily in the production, ensuring that each show was not just a concert but an event. Set designer Mark Ravitz created an environment which included what Bowie referred to as "high-tech columns" of transparent Perspex rising from the stage to the heavens, containing vast shafts of light topped with classical style joists apparently balanced on top. To the right of the stage was an enormous silvery crescent moon while to the left was a great hand, reaching towards it – reminiscent of the ape character Moon-Watcher in *2001: A Space Odyssey*, who similarly reached for the moon and wisdom. Bowie walked the stage Atlas-style with a large globe on his back which he would then launch into the crowd. Bouncing above their heads, it was inevitably pushed back to the stage, resulting in an entertaining and spectacular back and forth between star and fan. Some fans, lucky enough to attend a larger venue, were rewarded by the spectacle of a huge moon floating over the crowd and then opening to rain down smaller balloon moons on to the delighted fans.

The visual motifs were reinforced by a lighting rig that bathed the stage in a silvery, otherworldly glow, enhancing the ethereal quality of the performance. Despite the relative simplicity of the set design, the tour was notable for its use of cutting-edge technology. The lighting was state-of-the-art, and the sound system was designed to deliver crystal-clear audio in arenas and stadiums, ensuring that Bowie's voice could reach every corner of the venue. The visual aspect of the show was also enhanced by Diamond Vision video screens, a relatively new innovation at the time, which allowed fans in the back rows to see close-ups of Bowie and his band.

As ever, Bowie assembled an exceptional band for the Serious Moonlight Tour, including some of the most talented musicians of the era. Stevie Ray Vaughan was scheduled to join the tour and Bowie would certainly have benefitted from having the talented young player around to perform with him as he had on the album, but his drug use was a problem given Bowie's efforts to kick his own habits earlier in his career. There was also disagreement between him and Bowie's management about his fee and about whether Vaughan's band, Double Trouble, would be allowed to open some shows. In the end, Stevie did not join the tour, so Earl Slick, veteran of *Young Americans* and *Station to Station*, joined and learned the songs in a matter of days. Nile Rodgers had played rhythm guitar on the album but he was not joining the tour, so Carlos Alomar returned and took the role of band leader.

Completing the line-up were Carmine Rojas on bass; Tony Thompson of Chic on drums; Dave Lebolt on keyboards; and Frank Simms and George Simms on backing vocals. Their chemistry was evident from the first performance.

For the tour the arrangements of the classic hits from his extensive back catalogue were tailored to fit the upbeat, pop-oriented vibe of the tour. Even songs from Bowie's more experimental phases, such as '"Heroes"' or 'Ashes to Ashes', were given a more accessible, radio-friendly treatment. This approach was in keeping with the overall tone of the tour, which was less about pushing boundaries and more about celebrating Bowie's past while embracing his present success.

The set list varied somewhat from show to show, but it consistently featured a mix of tracks that spanned Bowie's career. In addition to the big hits from *Let's Dance*, Bowie included fan favourites like 'Rebel Rebel,' 'Fashion,' 'Golden Years,' and 'Fame.'

The tour was a massive success by any measure. It was Bowie's most extensive tour to date, covering 15 countries across 4 continents, with over 97 concerts performed. The tour grossed over $20 million, an astronomical figure at the time, and attracted nearly 3 million fans. Bowie performed in some of the largest venues in the world, including Madison Square Garden in New York, the Forum in Los Angeles, and Wembley Arena in London. Many of these shows sold out within hours, underscoring Bowie's now immense popularity.

Critically, the tour received overwhelmingly positive reviews. Bowie was praised for his charismatic stage presence, his vocal performance and the tightness of the band. The *New York Times* lauded the tour as "a triumph of showmanship," while *Rolling Stone* noted that Bowie had successfully balanced his artistic integrity with his newfound commercial appeal. Even those who had been sceptical of Bowie's more mainstream direction were won over by the energy and professionalism of the performances.

The Serious Moonlight Tour had a profound impact on both David Bowie's career and the broader cultural landscape. The culmination of his transformation from a cult figure into a global superstar cemented his status as one of the most important and influential artists of the 1980s, a position he would maintain for the rest of the decade. The tour also demonstrated Bowie's ability to adapt to the changing musical environment without compromising his unique artistic vision.

Moreover, the Serious Moonlight Tour set a new standard for live performances in the 1980s. Its combination of high production values, innovative technology and compelling performances became a template for future tours by other major artists. The tour is often credited with helping to redefine what a live rock concert could be, moving it closer to the realm of theatre and spectacle.

In hindsight, the Serious Moonlight Tour can be seen as a pivotal moment, one that not only celebrated his past achievements but also pointed the way toward his future endeavours.

Mick Ronson

Mark Plati

Emm Gryner and Mark Plati

Reeves Gabrels

Woody Woodmansey and Tony Visco

Carlos Alomar and David Bowie, Serious Moonlight

Robin Clark, Lea-Lorien and Carlos Alomar

Donny McCaslin and Nicholas Pegg

Andy, Woody, Donny, Carlos, Nick, Gail and Robin

Gail Ann Dorsey and Nick Smart

Jonathan Barnbrook, Donny McCaslin and Woody Woodmansey

Woody Woodmansey and John Cambridge

Nicholas Pegg,
Woody Woodmansey
and Nick Smart

Chapter 6
SAVIOUR MACHINE

Following the huge success of *Let's Dance* and the Serious Moonlight tour, the question became how to maintain the level of success. Bowie had received a large advance from EMI and naturally felt duty-bound to deliver. Another hit album was called for.

We have seen how Bowie sometimes felt he needed to break with the past – especially if he felt another person was beginning to have a large amount of influence or if the public was beginning to perceive the situation as such. Now, in 1984, on the back of his greatest commercial success, he seemed to feel the need to distance himself from Rodgers's influence and change course, as he had done so many times in the past.

Rodgers spoke at length about this to David Buckley, author of the excellent biography *Strange Fascination*. Rodgers explained that he'd had a very successful career long before he met Bowie. He'd had a hit with Bowie, sure, but he'd had bigger hits with Chic prior to his collaboration on *Let's Dance*. "Journalists would start asking questions like, 'How much did Nile have to do with this?'" Rodgers speaks of seeing interviews in which Bowie gives credit for high points in his career to Robert Fripp or Iggy Pop and little to him and says, "It seemed to be a conscious effort to distance himself from me."

By the late '90s, when Nile was speaking, things had changed. Bowie was now giving credit to Nile, but the message was that it was basically a Nile Rodgers album and that David had left him to it too much. Given the retrospective reassessment that *Let's Dance* went through in the '90s, when it began to be regarded as a creative low point, it may be that Bowie was seeking to explain the situation.

At the time, though, Bowie may have felt the need to change course to avoid being pigeonholed as a mainstream pop artist. Inviting Rodgers back might have risked repeating a formula, constraining Bowie's creative freedom. Bowie's desire to move in a new direction, both musically and artistically, meant that a fresh approach to production was necessary, leading him to collaborate with other producers, and in this case Derek Bramble and Hugh Padgham.

There is no doubt that, during the production of *Let's Dance*, Bowie took something of a back-seat role in the production process, allowing Rodgers to lead the way in shaping the album's sound. This inevitably meant that the record bore a strong imprint of Rodgers' style. For *Tonight*, Bowie chose to work with producers who had less influence over the overall sound of the album, ensuring that *Tonight* would be more reflective of his personal vision, even if it resulted in a less cohesive final product.

The mixed critical reception of *Let's Dance* might also have played a role in Bowie's decision. While the album was a massive commercial success, he perhaps hadn't realised that he might damage his standing as an artist with a dance album, regarded as more of a genre piece than a genre-defying work. Some critics and long-time Bowie fans clearly felt it was too polished and lacked the artistic depth of his earlier work. By not working with Rodgers again, Bowie could distance himself from these criticisms.

Bowie's decision may reflect his constant drive to evolve and challenge both himself and his audience, even if it meant moving away from a proven successful partnership. *Today* became his latest number one album in the UK, though it has turned out to be the one that most list compilers put at the bottom or in the bottom three of Bowie's "best" albums.

Fully five songs of the nine included on the album were co-written by his friend, Iggy Pop. "Some people cover the Rolling Stones. I cover Iggy Pop," said Bowie in explanation. 'Don't Look Down' had appeared on Iggy's *New Values* album, 'Tonight' and 'Neighborhood Threat' both appeared on the Bowie produced *Lust for Life*, while 'Dancing with the Big Boys' was a co-write between Bowie, Pop and the returning Carlos Alomar and features Pop on vocals. 'Tumble and Twirl' was another Bowie/Pop co-write.

Aside from the Iggy mini-album, there's a cover of an old Leiber/Stoller/Garfield track, 'I Keep Forgettin'' and another of the Beach Boys' 'God Only Knows', the latter of which is almost universally regarded as the lowest point of Bowie's illustrious career. This left two Bowie originals: 'Loving the Alien', a wonderful soaring epic which reflects Bowie's anger at the way in which religions fail to show to each other the love that they claim to believe in, and a protest about the ills that humanity has endured because of its faiths. The consensus seems to be that what could have been a Bowie classic is mired in '80s overproduction.

Finally, there's 'Blue Jean' and excellent piece of pop which according to Bowie is "a piece of sexist rock 'n' roll".

Supported by a comedic long-form video/ short film directed by Julien Temple called *Jazzin' for Blue Jean* it became a top ten single on both sides of the Atlantic.

The album's reviews were mixed but largely negative. It was called a "throwaway" by *Rolling Stone*. The influential teen mag *Smash Hits* felt it lacked direction. Charles Shaar Murray, in *NME* was again positive, praising its "mood and technique", while *Record Mirror* called it "a non-cohesive collection of both good and bad songs". It seems there was a lack of harmony in the studio, with Carlos Alomar – who had returned having been offered an acceptable deal this time – saying, plainly, that Bramble, the original producer, did not understand record production. Engineer Padgham was promoted to producer and asked to help clear up. Additionally, Bowie was again happy to come in with the ideas and let others put the album together. Given all of this, it's not hard to see why the album has come to be regarded as a creative nadir for Bowie. Although Bowie's practice had always been to collect ideas and influences, in the past he had combined and blended these to create original ideas and new perspectives. Here it seemed, the collection remained but the fusion and amalgamation were absent, leaving a feeling that the material of others is being reinterpreted rather than absorbed before being reborn anew. Perhaps it would have been a good idea to have asked Nile Rodgers back. Or Tony Visconti.

* * *

The longest break between albums in Bowie's career to date had been the three years between 1980's *Scary Monsters* and 1983's *Let's Dance*. Bowie was now about to equal that. He had much thinking to do. He'd had two of the biggest hit albums of his career and yet his reputation as an artist seemed to be in jeopardy. Bowie had realised he had lost his way. A period of reflection was called for.

This was not a break from music entirely. But as before, it was three years in which there was no new album and therefore no grand artistic statement. Bowie was reluctant to record another album at this time, despite EMI's prompting/pressuring. He recorded and released a single alongside the Pat Metheny Group, a rather smooth, slightly jazz, blink-and-you'll miss it piece called 'This is Not America' made for the Sean Penn film *The Falcon and the Snowman*, which did well to hit the top twenty in the UK and number seven in the US.

The year 1985 saw the triumph of Bowie's set at Live Aid, another demonstration of his rock god status which also spawned 'Dancing in the Street', the duet with Mick Jagger that was recorded after it became clear that they couldn't do a transatlantic live duet at the concert for technical reasons. More film work followed, including his appearance in *Absolute Beginners*, for which Bowie recorded the title track, earning him a number two hit in the UK with a song that many regard as one of his absolute finest. He took the lead in Jim Henson's *Labyrinth* which yielded another hit, 'Underground', and recorded 'When the Wind Blows' for the Raymond Briggs film of the same name, scoring another minor hit.

But time and record companies wait for no man and eventually it was time to deliver another album and world tour to promote it. He needed to make an album that would regain some of the artistic integrity that he had lost during what he came to call his "Phil Collins years". Later he would regret denigrating another artist, but his meaning was clear.

And he also needed to make an album that would be a hit and would justify a world tour. Was this an impossible task?

Never Let Me Down holds a unique place in his extensive discography, often viewed as a turning point and a symbol of a turbulent era in his career. The album's creation, motivations and reception offer a narrative that reflects Bowie's struggles with artistic identity, commercial pressures and his relationship with the music industry at large.

One of the primary motivations behind *Never Let Me Down* was Bowie's desire to reclaim his artistic integrity and assert himself as a serious musician once again. He was keenly aware of the criticisms levelled against his recent work and wanted to produce an album that was more personal, more in line with his earlier, groundbreaking material. Bowie envisioned *Never Let Me Down* as a return to form, an album that would re-establish his credibility as a songwriter and performer. This time, he would return to basics. Back to rock 'n' roll. When you're lost, go back to the start and take a new path from there.

Bowie would also involve himself in the recording process far more. Gone was the Bowie who left it to others to make his album while musically he contributed only vocals. On this record, he would play guitar, keyboards, Mellotron, Moog, synthesizer, harmonica and tambourine. Carlos returned, as he had on *Tonight,* as did Robin Clark, who had provided such distinctive vocals on *Young Americans.* Peter Frampton, who had known Bowie at school and whose father had taught art to both boys at Bromley Tech, came in to play lead guitar. This was to be an album that would follow on from *Scary Monsters.*

The making of *Never Let Me Down* was a complex and somewhat chaotic process. Long-time collaborator Carlos

Alomar played a significant role in the album's production and songwriting. The album was recorded primarily in Montreux, Switzerland, and New York City, with a variety of musicians contributing to its eclectic sound.

One of the defining characteristics of *Never Let Me Down* is its stylistic diversity. Bowie drew on a wide range of influences, including rock, pop, funk and electronic music. He was particularly interested in blending these genres to create something that was both contemporary and reflective of his own musical evolution. The album's production was ambitious, with Bowie and Alomar experimenting with new sounds and technologies, including the use of the Fairlight CMI, a digital synthesizer that allowed for complex sound manipulation.

Despite Bowie's high ambitions, the recording process was fraught with difficulties. There was a palpable tension between Bowie's desire for creative control and the commercial pressures imposed by his record label. EMI was eager for another hit album, and there was a significant push to make *Never Let Me Down* as accessible and radio-friendly as possible. This led to compromises in the production, with some tracks being overly polished and others lacking the rawness that Bowie had initially envisioned.

Thematically, the album was influenced by Bowie's reflections on his life and career at the time. He was disillusioned by the state of the world, particularly the political climate of the 1980s, marked by the Cold War. This sense of disillusionment is evident in tracks like 'Day-In Day-Out' and 'Time Will Crawl,' which touch on themes of social decay, political corruption, and the struggles of the working class. Bowie wanted the album to resonate with the times and to address contemporary issues that he felt passionate about.

When *Never Let Me Down* was released in April 1987, it received a mixed reception from critics and fans alike. While the album performed well commercially, reaching number 6 on the UK Albums Chart and number 34 on the US Billboard 200, it was met with considerable scepticism from the music press. Many critics felt that the album was unfocused and lacked the innovation that had characterised Bowie's earlier work.

One of the primary criticisms of *Never Let Me Down* was its production, which some described as overproduced and overly commercial. The album's polished sound, which was partly a result of the record label's influence, was seen as a departure from the edgier, more experimental style that Bowie was known for. Critics also pointed out that the album lacked the cohesive vision and thematic depth of his previous albums, making it feel disjointed and inconsistent.

Despite these criticisms, some tracks on the album were praised for their lyrical content and musicality. 'Time Will Crawl' and 'Never Let Me Down' were highlighted as stand-out tracks that showcased Bowie's songwriting prowess. The album's lead single, 'Day-In Day-Out,' also received attention for its commentary on social issues, although it failed to make a significant impact on the charts.

The album's accompanying tour, the Glass Spider Tour, was equally polarising. Bowie had envisioned the tour as a theatrical extravaganza, complete with elaborate stage designs, choreography and visual effects. This 1987 tour was the first time I saw Bowie live. I loved it. To be in the same space as Bowie – even an enormous space like Wembley Stadium or Cardiff Arms Park – and to be heading off on such an adventure with Andy, and my girlfriend, now wife, Kathrine was a treat.

Bowie put on a show full of spectacle. Toni Basil, who had choreographed the triumphant Diamond Dogs tour (and also had a novelty hit with 'Mickey') took on a similar task now. Many fans and critics felt that the spectacle overshadowed the music, leading to a perception that Bowie was more focused on style than substance. From my own vantage point, despite the enormous screens, I found it impossible to follow the action on the stage and simply enjoyed the songs.

The set itself featured an enormous spider with illuminated legs towering over the performance space and the show began with an extremely cool-looking Carlos, in his leather jacket, spiked hair and reflective glasses showing an additional pair of eyes above his head, taking centre stage and shredding on the guitar until Bowie's voice, in the manner of *Scary Monsters*' 'It's No Game' yells at him to "shut up!"

Carlos said of this:

> *The best costume was the spiky hair for Glass Spider. I ran up the ramp and for some reason my Achilles tendon snapped because of the incline. I still had to go on stage, so I took one of those 'Chuck Berry' hops onto the stage, but there was a dancer going to jump on my back to try to emulate a spider and as much as I tried to displace myself from the spot I was supposed to be in she flopped on. I was in such excruciating pain.*

Eventually, after Carlos's shredding, Bowie's voice booms out the spoken introduction to 'Glass Spider' and he, bedecked in red, is lowered from on high to the stage, speaking into a phone in an image reminiscent of the Diamond

Dogs tour. A highlight for many came in the encores when, weather permitting, Bowie would appear atop his arachnid overseer to perform 'Time', spreading his arms followed by a set of wings.

In between, it was difficult to follow what was happening. There were almost as many dancers as musicians and there was chanting and strange acrobatics. Maybe it would have looked great in a theatre but for a stadium – and perhaps also for an arena – the effect was lost and appeared overblown anyway.

In the years following its release, *Never Let Me Down* has been regarded as one of the weaker entries in Bowie's discography and it vies with *Tonight* as most fans' least favourite album.

In 2018, a reimagined version of the album was released as part of the *Loving the Alien (1983–1988)* box set. This new version, overseen by producer Mario J. McNulty, featured rerecorded and remixed tracks, aiming to strip away the overproduction that had marred the original release. The 2018 version received a more positive reception, with many praising it as a significant improvement over the original. A couple of years ago, I interviewed Bowie's long-time drummer Sterling Campbell, who worked on the project and said:

> *Mario McNulty and I got to reimagine Never Let Me Down. That was fun. Some people like the way it was, and I understand. But it was fun. It was fun, like to be... to hear David's tracks pulled apart, trying to make something out of it. Really kinda hard when we didn't have him there, even though we did that originally. David took one of the tracks and he wanted to redo the record. That was*

his plan at some point to do that. That's a hard thing to do if he's not there.

Never Let Me Down remains a fascinating chapter in David Bowie's career. It is an album that reflects the struggles of an artist trying to balance creativity with commercial demands, and it offers insight into Bowie's mindset during a turbulent period in his life. While it may not be as celebrated as his other works, *Never Let Me Down* continues to be a subject of interest and debate among Bowie fans, serving perhaps as a reminder of the complexities and contradictions that define his musical legacy.

The album that was supposed to be a back-to-basics return to form which would simultaneously maintain his superstar status had done neither.

Perhaps he hadn't gone back to basics *enough*! What was needed was a Saviour Machine!

* * *

Bowie clearly realised that he *really* needed to go back to basics. He even considered quitting music to focus on other artistic endeavours. By the end of the Glass Spider tour, he reputedly burned one of the sets to the ground in a field. While that story may be apocryphal, he was more than ready to put his recent past behind him.

Bass player Tony Sales, along with his drummer brother Hunt, had played in Iggy Pop's band during the period when Bowie was producing them and would go on to have a much bigger involvement with Bowie. Immediately after the tour ended, Bowie had a chance encounter with Tony. As Tony told me:

> *I was out – having dinner or something – and somebody said to me, "Did you know David was having a wrap party for the Glass Spider Tour?"*
>
> *I said: "No, I didn't", and they said, "You should stop by and say hi to him." So, I showed up at this address which was a club in town. I walked downstairs and David was sitting there on the floor against the wall and there were people dancing around and he looked like he wasn't having too much fun, so I walked up to him.*
>
> *I said: "Hey buddy, get up!", you know. And he said "Tony!! Tony, I was just thinking about you! I wanna talk to you about something!!" So, I said, "OK." So, we went back to the hotel and said that he wanted to put a band together. And I said, "Should I call the drummer?" He said, "Call the drummer." Then he said: "I've this guitar player I want you to meet. His name's Reeves. I want you to meet him. I did a couple of things with him but I think you'll really enjoy his playing" and then he said: "Let's go and rock", and I said: "OK, let's do it!" And a week later we were in Switzerland cutting the first album.*

Bowie clearly wasn't in the mood for wasting time. He had a drummer and bass player – and a guitar player, Reeves Gabrels, in mind.

Reeves now takes up the story about the genesis of the band that would become Tin Machine:

> *I met him in 1987 at the first American outside show of The Glass Spider Tour. At that time, I was sharing a house with three other guys who were Harvard graduates, music school graduates. It was a pretty interesting cross section; we had a band called The Dark. David would have fitted*

right in! His interests and reasons for doing things were just like the rest of my friends who were all smart artists. When David and I first met we realised we were listening to same type of music – Miles Davis, the Pixies, Led Zeppelin bootlegs, Cream bootlegs and John Lee Hooker.

He had a great sense of humour, that was one of the many joys of it. I met him because my ex-wife was working as his press rep on the USA leg of The Glass Spider Tour. David called me while he was on set of The Last Temptation of Christ. He left me a message on my phone; it was maybe only the third time I had spoken to him in person. Hearing his message at two in the morning while I was soaking wet having travelled back from a gig in the snow and probably drunk – it was very strange!

It seems that Sarah Gabrels had given a demo of Reeves' playing to Bowie, who was mightily impressed.

So, Bowie now had all the ingredients he needed to do the unthinkable. Faced with a future of either accepting that his best years were behind him and therefore singing his old hits cabaret style in Vegas, or doing something really unexpected, he chose the latter and formed a band.

Work on the album began immediately. Albums take a little time to write and record, of course. So the first time the world saw Bowie and Reeves together was at the show Intruders at the Palace in which David appeared with the avant-garde dance group La La La Human Steps, led by the renowned Canadian choreographer Édouard Lock. The performance took place on 1 July, 1988, at the Dominion Theatre in London, as part of a benefit concert for the London Institute of Contemporary Arts.

This collaboration was characteristic of Bowie's deep

interest in integrating various art forms into his work, pushing the boundaries of rock performance by merging it with contemporary dance. It was therefore the perfect vehicle to begin to remind his audience that his creative edge had not been blunted. La La La Human Steps was known for its physically demanding and emotionally intense style, characterised by rapid, intricate movements and a raw, kinetic energy. This avant-garde approach resonated with Bowie at a time when he was seeking new ways to express his music visually and theatrically.

The centrepiece of the performance was 'Look Back in Anger,' a track from Bowie's 1979 album *Lodger*. Bowie performed the song live on stage while the dancers, including the celebrated Louise Lecavalier, delivered a stunning interpretation of the music through their frenetic choreography. The interaction between Bowie and the dancers created a powerful and surreal atmosphere, blending the worlds of rock and contemporary dance in the most provocative way.

Intruders at the Palace stands out as a reminder of Bowie's willingness to experiment and collaborate across artistic disciplines, reinforcing his reputation as an artist who constantly sought to evolve and challenge conventional boundaries. The performance was a one-off event but left a lasting impact, demonstrating Bowie's commitment to art in its many forms and his ability to connect with audiences through unexpected and daring collaborations.

So far, so good.

The album needed a producer and Bowie wanted a break from the past. The idea now was that this wasn't David Bowie's band but simply a band of which he happened to be a member. Although it might be tricky to convince the world of this, the idea of the band was that it was a four-way democracy. Therefore, a new producer was needed. That man was Tim Palmer, who explains how his involvement came about:

> *During the recording of The Mission albums [which he produced] I had met the Cult who had come into the studio to meet with the band. Around this time Reeves Gabrels was working on sketches and ideas for the new David Bowie album with David in Switzerland and they were trying to work out who to collaborate with as producer and engineer. Reeves reached out to his friend Billy Duffy, the guitar player from the Cult, and legend has it that Billy put forward my name as an idea. So, I ended up getting contacted in London from David Bowie's manager. We set up a phone call for me to have a chat with David and Reeves about the new album, and the rest is history.*

So, the band was all together and now it was time to strip things back to basics. In the early days of their working together, Bowie candidly told Reeves that having to produce hits for EMI was "killing" him. The Tin Machine project was born of their discussions which focused on many subjects, notable art, but also on the need to simply write and play rock 'n' roll.

Gabrels had argued with David about making it a band project. To Andy and me, he said, "When we started writing songs for that album, we always knew it was going to be released as part of David's contract with EMI." To biographer Mark Spitz, he admitted, "I argued with David that I didn't think it was a good idea to make it a band, but he needed to make something that would fall on the barbed wire fence of expectation."

"But I wanted play on a David Bowie record," he told me and Andy. "I wanted to be David Bowie's guitarist. I didn't want to be in a band, so I dragged my feet on it. But I gave in because they outvoted me!"

Another guitarist would also be needed, and the clear choice was Kevin Armstrong. Kevin had played on the *Absolute Beginners* session. Mysteriously, he received an invitation to attend a session with a "Mr X". Kevin guessed it must be someone noteworthy – otherwise, why the mystery? He told me:

> *I had no idea who was going to be there. There was some talk amongst the musicians about who it was likely to be and I think he was on the list of guesses, but it was still a marvellous surprise when he walked in. I remember feeling that this was a really special moment for me and I hoped we could do something good for him. As it turned out, I was the guy who he picked to do more work with him over a period of 10 years, so he obviously liked something I could bring to the table. I did Iggy Pop's Blah Blah Blah album with him and the first Tin Machine album and tour as well as contributing to the Outside album.*

Kevin had also played at the Intruders at the Palace performance and at Live Aid. Now he took his place with the band.

As recording began, in Nassau, it was clear that this was going to different from any project the five of them had worked on in the past. The band did indeed work on a democratic basis. It was five guys together against the world. They decided to record live – that is, with all the band members and the singer performing simultaneously.

By the late '80s, this was not at all the way things were done — and hadn't been since the '60s or perhaps the early '70s, and required a different approach to recording and sound separation and a large dose of nerve from the sound engineers. For the first time since *"Heroes"*, Bowie improvised lyrics and the band encouraged him to "stand by them" rather than rethink and adjust later on, as had been his previous habit.

Bowie's collaboration with Gabrels was particularly significant. Known for his wildly creative virtuosity, Gabrels brought a fresh, abrasive approach to guitar playing that contrasted dramatically with the more commercial and radio-friendly sounds of the '80s. As much as Bowie wanted and needed to return to basics, it was Reeves's influence as much as Bowie's that was key in driving the band towards a raw, hard-edged sound. While this was a deliberate move away from the highly produced sound of Bowie's recent records, Gabrels added a layer of innovative turbulence which, at its best, lifted the product beyond mere garage rock.

Tin Machine is often described as a hard rock album, but this label only partially captures its essence. The record channels a range of influences, from the punk rock energy of the Stooges and the Velvet Underground to the experimental noise of Sonic Youth and is characterised by distorted guitars, aggressive rhythms and a generally raw production style.

The album opens with 'Heaven's in Here,' a slow-building track that introduces the band's gritty sound. Gabrels's guitar work is front and centre, with his jagged riffs and unconventional solos setting the tone. Bowie's vocals are more restrained than in his solo work, blending into the music rather than dominating it. This collaborative spirit permeates the entire album, with each band member contributing to the overall sound.

Perhaps one of the most notable tracks on the album is 'Under the God,' which was also released as a single. It's a fast-paced, punk-infused song with politically charged lyrics that criticise racism and right-wing extremism. The track's directness and urgency stood in stark contrast to the more abstract and poetic lyrics Bowie was known for. In 'Under the God', Bowie's voice is angry and confrontational, echoing the raw energy of the band's instrumentation.

'Prisoner of Love', another standout track, showcases a different side of *Tin Machine*. While still rooted in rock, it's a more melodic song with a strong chorus and a slightly more polished sound. However, it maintains the band's edge, with Gabrels' guitar work providing a counterpoint to the more conventional structure of the song.

Lyrically, *Tin Machine* reflects Bowie's disillusionment with both the music industry and the broader political landscape. The late 1980s was a time of significant global change, with the Cold War winding down and social tensions rising. Bowie's lyrics on the album are more direct and less abstract than in much of his earlier work. Bowie appeared to have developed the desire to speak out on issues that concerned him, a quality that was also characteristic of *Never Let Me Down*.

A case in point is 'Crack City' – a scathing critique of urban decay and drug culture, with Bowie delivering lines like "Don't look at me you fuckhead / This nation's turning blue / Its stink it fouls the highways / Its filth it sticks like glue" with biting sarcasm. The song's gritty subject matter is matched by its harsh, driving instrumentation, but was this what the world needed from Bowie? The artist who had once stood apart from the world he inhabited, allowing his audience to look upon it with new eyes and consider its absurdities and possibilities as if it were their playground – their world to consider and shape – was now reduced to chants that sounded like they belonged on the terraces of the Stretford End.

Another track, 'I Can't Read', delves into themes of alienation and existential angst. The song's slow, almost plodding pace creates a sense of despair, with Bowie singing about the inability to connect with the world around him. The minimalist lyrics and repetitive structure reflect the monotony and frustration of modern life. 'Video Crime', meanwhile, takes aim at the increasing influence of media and technology on society. The song critiques how television and video had begun to shape people's perceptions of reality, a theme that Bowie would explore further in his later work. The track's mechanical rhythm and cold, detached vocals enhance the sense of dehumanisation Bowie sought to convey.

Live the band was as chaotic and powerful as one might imagine. Tony Sales told me:

> *Tin Machine really was… we really were avant-garde compared with anybody now. I remember doing improvisational stuff every night. You know, no two shows were the same. We would start off with a base, of course – the foundation of what the song was but then we would change along the way, so it was never the same. And David was doing poetry every night. It was incandescent, you know. It was so special to me that I … I was so enthusiastic about it. Every day we were doing a gig and it was great working*

> *with David, too. I hadn't worked with him for about ten years. It was great to work with him. It was real open spirit, supporting project.*

It was remarkably loud, sweaty and cacophonous. It was both madly creative and boisterously mind-numbing.

Upon its release, *Tin Machine* received mixed reviews from critics and fans alike. Many were unsure how to react to Bowie's new direction, with some praising the album for its boldness and others dismissing it as a misstep. The raw, unpolished sound was a far cry from the Bowie of the '70s and early '80s, and some listeners found it difficult to reconcile this new, band-oriented approach with their expectations of Bowie as a solo artist.

Commercially, the album performed moderately well, reaching number 3 on the UK Albums Chart and number 28 on the US Billboard 200. The singles 'Under the God' and 'Prisoner of Love' also had limited success, reflecting the album's polarising nature.

In hindsight, *Tin Machine* can be seen as a necessary reinvention for Bowie. It allowed him to strip away the excesses of his previous work and reconnect with the raw energy that had driven his early career. The album's collaborative nature also helped to rejuvenate Bowie: working with a band allowed him to share the creative load and explore new musical ideas.

Tin Machine may not have been the commercial or critical success that Bowie's earlier albums were, but it did play a role in his artistic evolution. By stepping away from the expectations of being a solo artist and embracing the collaborative nature of a band, Bowie was able to rediscover his passion for music. The album's raw, unfiltered sound and its direct, often confrontational lyrics were a clear break from the past, signalling a new chapter in Bowie's career.

Perhaps *Tin Machine* is best regarded as a manifesto rather than an album. Bowie needed to move as far away as possible from the overproduced, overly commercial albums of the '80s and enter the next decade renewed. To be fair, 'I Can't Read', is rightly regarded as a classic Bowie track, and it is the only one to have survived the era – both as a live one and as a song later rerecorded by a solo David Bowie.

Bowie the collector had indeed collected the musicians and influences he needed and repurposed them for his own needs. Overall, *Tin Machine* may have been the album he needed to make, but it may not have been the album his audience needed to hear.

So, Bowie had made a decisive break with his past. He had refused to play a single old song on the tour and the album contained nothing that anyone would recognise as Bowie. At last, he'd thrown off the shackles of the old albums and his superstar trappings. What would he do next?

A solo greatest hits tour, of course!

* * *

Bowie may be regarded as the arch changeling whose next move can never be predicted, but few would have thought this would be his next step. For fans it was, at least, a sign that Bowie was paying attention to his solo career alongside that of his band.

There was an explanation for this, of course. The Massachusetts record company Rykodisc had put together a beautifully packaged box set of Bowie material for the period from 1969 to 1980, called Sound + Vision. Part career retrospective, part sampler for a rerelease programme for his older albums, Ryko suggested it would be great to support the box set and upcoming releases with a Greatest Hits tour. Bowie was game, but on one condition – that he retire these hit songs after the tour. He would instead build up a new repertoire in the coming years and perform those songs instead.

He would also use a telephone poll to invite people to suggest songs for him to play, promising to abide by the results – although of course, the results were predictable.

Visually, the tour was stunning. An enormous mesh screen could be lowered in front of the band onto which images and movies could be projected. We were treated to a God-like Bowie looking down on the stage as the real Bowie sat below strumming 'Space Oddity' on a 12-string in much the same way he had in folk clubs and his own arts lab more than two decades earlier – save of course that he was now placed in context by the enormous presence that *David Bowie* had become.

Musically, the tour featured a stripped-down, three-piece band: Bowie on vocals and guitar, Adrian Belew on guitar, Erdal Kızılçay on bass, Rick Fox playing keyboards and Michael Hodges on drums. This was about as minimalist as it could get and there were some songs which sounded somewhat thin – 'Young Americans' without the saxophone, for example.

The tour spanned 108 dates across the globe, covering North America, Europe, Asia and South America. The Sound + Vision tour was both a celebration of Bowie's past and a signal of his future direction, marking the end of one era and the beginning of another.

Another Tin Machine album followed, plus a tour and live album. There were highs and lows and the commercial performance of each was poorer than the last. The drug problems of Hunt Sales made things difficult on the second tour and it was clear that things had run their course.

But Bowie emerged renewed. From now on and for some while, each new album would be hailed as a return to form or, as the cliché now has it, "his best since *Scary Monsters*".

Black Tie White Noise was Bowie's first solo studio album in six years. Produced by Nile Rodgers, who had previously collaborated with Bowie on the hugely successful *Let's Dance*, the album was experimental and fresh. The Sound + Vision tour had helped to remind the public of who Bowie was and what he could do, and when *Black Tie White Noise* was released in April 1993, it reached number one on the UK Albums Chart, signalling Bowie's return to the forefront of popular music.

The album was heavily influenced by Bowie's personal life, particularly his marriage to Iman in 1992. Whereas in the past Bowie had sought out uncomfortable situations and even personal misery in order to improve his writing, most notably in California in 1974, themes of love and marriage are now at the fore, reflecting Bowie's evolving world view and personal contentment. The title track addresses racial tension in the aftermath of the 1992 Los Angeles riots, blending elements of funk, jazz and electronic music to create a sound that was distinctly modern and yet somehow still rooted in Bowie's earlier work.

Musically, *Black Tie White Noise* is a fusion of genres. Bowie draws from his past but embraces new influences, including house music, which was gaining popularity in the early 1990s. Tracks like 'Jump They Say' reflect this blend, its electronic beats and saxophone solos combining as Bowie does at his best, to break new ground. The song, inspired by the death of Bowie's half-brother Terry, deals with themes of mental illness and societal pressure. This was Bowie's re-engagement with the mainstream, yet on his own terms.

Later in 1993, Bowie released *The Buddha of Suburbia*, a soundtrack album for the BBC television adaptation of Hanif Kureishi's novel of the same name. The album is now regarded more as a bona fide Bowie album than a soundtrack. Unlike *Black Tie White Noise*, this album was not designed for mainstream success, but rather as an experimental and introspective work. Despite its relatively low profile at the time of release, *The Buddha of Suburbia* has since been recognised as one of Bowie's most underrated albums.

The album's title track is a reflective piece that blends rock with ambient and world music influences, playing on the novel's themes of cultural identity and the search for meaning in suburban life, with Bowie delivering one of his most nuanced vocal performances. The song's layered production, incorporating sitars and electronic elements, showcases Bowie's interest in blending traditional and modern sounds.

Unlike traditional soundtracks, *The Buddha of Suburbia* features only a few tracks that were directly used in the TV series, with most of the album consisting of new compositions, which partly explains its retrospective status as a Bowie studio album. Bowie saw this as an opportunity to experiment with different styles and revisit some of his earlier influences. The album includes everything from the ambient, Brian Eno-inspired 'South Horizon' to the jazz-inflected 'Bleed Like a Craze, Dad', demonstrating, in contrast to Tin Machine, his new-found more eclectic approach.

But it was with the return of Reeves Gabrels that the renaissance really began.

Reeves had passed on an offer to play with Bowie on the Sound + Vision tour, feeling that to have half of Tin Machine on stage would confuse matters. He played on one track on *Black Tie White Noise* and didn't appear on *The Buddha of Suburbia* but returned in earnest for 1995's *1. Outside* when Reeves at last became what he'd hoped he would be when he joined Tin Machine – David Bowie's guitar player.

Having reunited with Nile Rodgers to good effect for *Black Tie White Noise,* Bowie now reunited with Brian Eno for the *1. Outside* album. Unlike the Berlin Trilogy, Eno was the producer this time, alongside David Richards who had also handled production on *Never Let Me Down* and *The Buddha of Suburbia*. Others returned, too. Mike Garson, who had first played with Bowie in 1973 on the Ziggy Stardust tour, was back on piano and would remain into the next century. Sterling Campbell, the drummer from *Black Tie White Noise* returned and would also remain a long-term fixture. Also returning on bass was Erdal Kızılçay, and this was also the first album since 1987 to have featured Carlos Alomar on rhythm guitar, who returned for the last of the sessions. Previously, on *Black Tie White Noise*, Mick Ronson had returned to play guitar on Cream's 'I Feel Free', a song which the Spiders had covered live back in the day. Clearly Bowie was in the mood for revisiting the past and working with old friends.

The return of Eno signalled a more experimental approach, naturally, and Reeves Gabrels was fully able to bring his wild virtuosity to the project. Eno's Oblique Strategies cards were back. David Buckley reports that one instruction to Sterling Campbell was, 'You are the disgruntled ex-member of a South African rock band. Play the notes you weren't allowed to play.' Garson was told, 'You are a soothsayer and town crier in a society where all media networks have tumbled down.' Others were given other characters to play as in the studio. As part of the experimental atmosphere, Bowie set up an easel in the studio and spent the first few days painting. Bowie's cut ups technique was back in earnest as well, aided by a computer program which could mix and arrange the fragmented lines in moments. Bowie the collector was using everything he knew and plenty that was new.

Garson was extremely positive about the way the sessions went, saying that it was one of the most creative environments he had experienced. Like Belew before him during the *Lodger* sessions, Garson was asked to simply play without knowing anything about the piece he was playing, including the key. Reeves Gabrels remembers a different vibe, telling Dylan Jones that he had turned up a week before the start of the sessions and when the others arrived, they started to jam, but this was difficult in the studio because Brian Eno didn't play an instrument – his instrument was his ideas. However, Sterling Campbell was clearly happy, recalling breakfasting with Eno daily and then jamming for hours while Bowie painted. Much of the album was assembled from these jams – 'The Hearts Filthy Lesson' is one example.

Eno writes in his diary of the time, "In the studio here we're doing just about the exact opposite. My brows wrinkle frequently and I become the sculptor to David's tendency to paint. I keep trying to cut back, strip them to something tense and taut, while he keeps throwing new colours on the canvas." He adds, diplomatically, "It's a good duet".

Later, Eno was to say, "The interesting place is not chaos and it's not total coherence. It's somewhere on the cusp of those two." As ever, he took the role of disrupting things if the studio jams started to turn into predicable blues workouts.

The album that emerged is thematically dense and rich with narrative, marking Bowie's return to a darker, more experimental sound. *1. Outside* explored a fragmented world where art, crime and identity intertwine in unsettling ways. The album's themes are numerous and layered, encompassing dystopian visions of the future, the role of art in society, the fragmentation of identity, and the nature of time and memory – and revolve around the ritualist "art murder" of a 14-year-old girl and the subsequent investigation by detective Nathan Adler.

One of the central themes of *1. Outside* is the vision of a future world where societal norms have broken down and urban decay is rampant. The album is set in a near-future 1999, a time where traditional boundaries between art and crime have blurred. The concept of Art Crime becomes a central narrative, with the idea that extreme and grotesque acts, including murder, are now being committed in the name of art. This dystopian setting reflects Bowie's ongoing interest in the dark undercurrents of society, and his vision of a future where humanity's obsessions with technology and sensationalism have led to moral decay.

Tracks like 'The Motel' and 'No Control' delve into this bleak environment, where characters wander through a chaotic world, seeking meaning in a landscape that has lost its moral compass. Bowie's lyrics paint a picture of a society on the edge, grappling with the consequences of its own excesses and the loss of human connection.

Another prominent theme in *1. Outside* is the exploration of art's role in society, particularly in the context of a world where boundaries between reality and performance have dissolved. Bowie, through his various characters on the album, questions what it means to create art in a world where artifice and reality are indistinguishable – this from the man who brought artifice to rock 'n' roll with Ziggy Stardust. The album's central character, Detective Nathan Adler, investigates a ritualistic murder that is presented as a piece of art. This scenario raises questions about the nature of art and the moral responsibilities of the artist, blurring the lines between the role of art to either reflect the horrors of the world, or instigate them.

In 'I'm Deranged' and 'A Small Plot of Land,' Bowie explores the idea that art has become disconnected from its original purpose, serving instead as a vehicle for violence and chaos. The artist, once a creator of beauty and meaning, becomes complicit in the darker aspects of human nature.

1. Outside also delves deeply into the theme of identity, particularly the fragmentation and multiplicity of self. Bowie, known for his various alter egos throughout his career, takes this exploration to new heights, presenting a cast of characters, each representing different facets of the human psyche. The album blurs the lines between these characters, making it difficult to discern where one ends and another begins.

The character of Leon Blank, for instance, is a young artist who may or may not be the killer, embodying the confusion and instability of identity in the modern world.

The song 'The Hearts Filthy Lesson' captures this sense of fragmentation, with its chaotic, overlapping vocals and disjointed narrative. Bowie suggests that in a world where identity is constantly being constructed and deconstructed, the search for a coherent self is increasingly elusive.

The album grapples with the nature of time and memory, and their roles in shaping our understanding of reality. The album's narrative is nonlinear, with Bowie shifting between past, present and future, creating a disorienting sense of temporal dislocation. This reflects the postmodern idea that time is not a straightforward progression but a series of overlapping and fragmented moments.

Reeves Gabrels brought a distinctive, avant-garde edge to the album, helping to create its dark, experimental tone. His contributions were not limited to guitar work; Gabrels was deeply involved in the album's creative process, influencing its overall direction and production. Gabrels' guitar work on *1. Outside* is characterised by its dissonant, textural approach, blending traditional rock elements with unconventional sounds. He employed a range of techniques, from aggressive, distorted riffs to ambient, atmospheric effects, which added to the album's sense of unease and complexity. Unshackled from the constraints of the Tin Machine format, Gabrels could shine.

1. Outside is an album that defies easy categorisation, both musically and thematically. Its exploration of dystopian futures, the role of art, the fragmentation of identity, and the nature of time and memory make it Bowie's most eclectic work to date. The album had been envisaged as a double or triple CD called *Leon*, and there was more than enough material, but it was difficult to persuade a record company to release such a work, so Bowie re-entered the studio, with Carlos Alomar among others, to edit, rerecord and add some parts in order to make a more cohesive single album – which still weighed in at a hefty 75 minutes.

The tour that followed was minimalist in presentation and extensive in duration, beginning in September 1995 and ending in the same month the following year. The boundary blurring of the studio was carried over onto the stage as support band Nine Inch Nails did not leave the stage after their set but rather were joined by Bowie for a duet and then left, leaving Bowie to perform his solo set.

Sterling Campbell couldn't join the tour as he explained when I interviewed him in 2023:

> *It was really like circumstance when David was ready to go out on the road. He was really not ready to go out on the road for a while. Even with Outside. He said he was going to do it but didn't say when. It kind of went on, so I didn't think it was going to happen. So, I got involved with another band [Soul Asylum] and I committed to it, so by the time he asked, I had to like… it's hard to imagine; I had to turn it down. But I made a commitment to the other band. So, I told him about my childhood friend, Zack.*

Thus began Zachary Alford's tenure, which would alternate with Sterling's for many years to come. Fun fact: as well as alternating in Bowie's band, the pair have alternated in the B-52s since 1992.

For the tour, Bowie largely stuck to his pledge not to perform old favourites. While a few older songs, even singles, were performed – 'Boys Keep Swinging' and 'Scary Monsters' for example, the set was largely drawn from recent material and some less obvious older songs.

For his part, Carlos Alomar only played the first leg of the tour. He told David Buckley that he'd found Bowie inaccessible, which he put down to David's recent marriage. "I found myself extremely lonely," adding, "It just became a question of 'When can I leave?'"

A few years ago, Carlos was feeling more diplomatic, although he hints at some reasons why things may have been difficult:

> *That is actually why I left Bowie. I was doing the Outside tour and it was really, really going well. It was different. David wanted more experimental music based on things that were in the computer, so he got this keyboard guy in [Peter Schwartz] and he was made the band leader. Because he was the band leader, he kind of felt I had been looked over. He may have felt that I felt resentment because he was now the band leader. He didn't really understand my nature and the fact I'm a Buddhist and I don't really care.*
>
> *The tour was good, but we had to put these earphones on because we they were feeding us music that's on track. So, nobody looks at you. In the old days we used to feed off each other. So, when the drummer hit his drum hard, I would play a louder note and the bass player would add an extra action. So, by the end of a tour in the old days we had this amazing rapport and now is the time we should record the album at the end of the tour.*
>
> *No... on this one (the Outside tour) it stayed the same because we were playing to a clock, you know what I mean? A little boring. Then ... my wife Robin got sick. She had back problems and had to have an operation. It was a serious situation. It happened just as we were about to go*

> *from America to Europe and I got the news and David saw me the day after I got off the phone. I didn't know what to do, I was not about to go anywhere but home. David said, "What the fuck are you doing here, go home!" There was no goodbye, there was no nothing. After the tour was finished there were albums that he did when he called me in to do additional work, but quite honestly by then the spark of originality was gone and you listen to a song and you think I don't want to play on that, you're not needing me on that one. It wasn't really the same, you know.*
>
> *I was called in for a "sweetening session". You know when everything is mostly done but not quite finished, so I was asked to add to the tracks, which I did. That's what I did with McCartney too. I was asked to do a sweetening session, but I ended up doing a whole damn album.*

Morrissey, who was opening the UK shows, apparently thought it would be more of a fifty-fifty thing and became disgruntled, saying to audiences: "I'm the support act," and "Don't worry. David will be along in a minute." He suddenly left the tour before a show in Aberdeen leaving a perplexed David to explain on a Scottish TV show that he'd simply received a message to say that Morrissey wasn't going to be working that night. Bowie then promised the TV audience that he would be putting on a great show. For his part, Morrissey spent the next few years criticising Bowie for being irrelevant at every opportunity.

As we have seen, many of the musicians who had joined Bowie latterly and remained for this album and tour remained with him for the rest of his career. Another such was Gail Ann Dorsey, who joined as bass player for this tour. Her striking look, with cropped hair and no shoes, seemed to sum up the spirit of the tour and, as Zack Alford told Mark Spitz, "Aside from her magnificent voice, she played only the fattest most tasteful basslines. She is a knight in shining armour. That's why we call her 'Dame' Dorsey."

The only downside for Gail was that she had joined at a time when Bowie had retired much of his back catalogue. Gail remained with Bowie almost to the end, and Bowie did gradually reintroduce many of his older hits, but there was always one thing missing for Gail, as she explained:

> *He didn't really want to do anything from Young Americans and that's my favourite Bowie album. I love that album. I don't know why he wouldn't play those songs. I tried to get it out of him. We used to rehearse 'Win' when he wasn't around and we decided we would play it when he walked into rehearsals in the hope he would agree to play it. We would break into it during rehearsals too and he would look around and give us a look to say, "STOP IT!" He really didn't want to sing those songs – they conjured something different for him but I don't know what it was.*
>
> *For me it was very frustrating because his vocals on that record was some of the greatest singing I have ever heard in my life. I played that record to death when it came out. I remember thinking, Who is this man who can sing like this? Incredible singing, the whole album. Oh my god Carlos, Carlos Alomar, amazing contribution to that album. His wife Robin, what a voice!*

In common with most of the band, Reeves continued with Bowie on the following two albums. The first of which, 1997's *Earthling* is often regarded as Bowie's drum and bass album, although it is far more. As Paolo Hewitt notes,

Bowie brought his best Anthony Newley voice – one that he hadn't used since his pre-fame mock music hall days.

Earthling is often seen as Bowie's most overt engagement with the contemporary sounds of the 1990s, particularly the burgeoning electronic music scene. Released in 1997, the album was heavily influenced by drum and bass, jungle, and industrial music, blending these genres with rock in a way that was both futuristic and edgy. Gabrels' contributions were central to this fusion of styles, as his guitar work provided a bridge between the electronic beats and Bowie's rock sensibilities.

Gabrels' guitar on *Earthling* is characterised by its aggressive, textured sound, which often mimicked or complemented the electronic elements of the album. 'Little Wonder' and 'Dead Man Walking', for example, feature his use of digital effects, distortion and unusual tunings, creating a sonic palette that was both innovative and seemed to match the album's high-energy, electronic foundation. Perhaps most of all, his ability to merge guitar with electronic textures without losing the organic feel of rock was key to *Earthling*'s success as a genre-blending album.

Gabrels also contributed to the songwriting on *Earthling*, co-writing several tracks, including 'Dead Man Walking' and 'Battle for Britain (The Letter).' His input helped shape the album's themes of alienation, and technology, with his guitar work often reflecting the fragmented, frenetic pace of contemporary life that Bowie was exploring. Gabrels' influence on *Earthling* extended beyond his technical skills, as his experimental mindset and willingness to push boundaries were integral to the album's avant-garde approach.

In contrast to the high-energy, electronically infused

Earthling, Bowie's next original album, *Hours*, released in 1999, marked a return to a more introspective and melodic style. This shift in tone also reflected a different aspect of Gabrels' influence, as his guitar work on *Hours* was more subdued and emotionally resonant, complementing the album's themes of reflection and nostalgia.

On *Hours*, Gabrels' guitar playing took on a more lyrical and atmospheric quality, supporting the album's more song-oriented structure. Tracks like 'Thursday's Child' and 'Survive' showcase Gabrels' ability to create mood and texture with his guitar, using clean tones and subtle effects to enhance the emotional depth of Bowie's songwriting. His solos on these tracks are restrained yet expressive, serving the songs rather than overwhelming them, which was in keeping with the album's introspective nature.

Reeves was also deeply involved in the songwriting process for *Hours*, co-writing every track on the album. His contributions helped shape the album's more traditional rock sound, resulting in an album that, while less radical than its predecessor, was rich in emotional nuance and melodic sophistication.

Gabrels' influence on *Hours* is also evident in the way the album integrates modern production with classic songwriting. While the album looked back to Bowie's earlier work in some respects, Gabrels ensured that it still felt contemporary and relevant, balancing the reflective lyrics with a fresh, updated sound.

In truth, Bowie had never before formed a partnership the way he did with Reeves Gabrels, although the partnership tends to be under-recognised. When Andy and I interviewed him, Andy mentioned his songwriting saying, "I know you wrote many songs with Bowie – over seventy!"

Reeves replied simply, "You must be the only one who does." He went on to describe how the partnership worked:

> *There was no process when we wrote songs together. I never thought of myself as a songwriter until I worked with David. There was no formula. With the Outside album David, Brian (Eno) and I would fax each other ideas for songs.*
>
> *Sometimes David would compose on a piano and use a tape recorder, which he would pause when he needed to and then he would sing, then play until he had figured out the next part and then he would release pause and carry on with the parts he had just figured out. When we wrote for Earthling he sat together with loops I had made, we would play guitars over the loops. We would just jam over the loops until we hit on an idea.*

Hours, Reeves decided, was to be the final album he played on, however. Bowie was a little dismayed and asked why. "I'm going to play with children my own age," he explained – which upset Bowie somewhat. Never before in his solo career had Bowie formed such a complete partnership. The pair even shared writing credits on all the songs they made, Lennon and McCartney style, no matter which of the two wrote them.

Reeves expanded on this in our interview:

> *There were several reasons. I was very happy with the music we produced, it was never made to have a hit single or album. I was always on the art being the most important thing. It wasn't about money either; at that time I was probably only just above the poverty line. I might be eating*

> *a cheese sandwich for the fourth time in four days, but you've got the art and you've done what you wanted to do. When I was at school my Mum bought me Ziggy Stardust. What was driving David was the art, always the art. He wanted to create some stir and outrage. It's different from doing it for the money.*

Towards the end of the interview, I recalled the observation by Nicholas Pegg, author of *The Complete David Bowie*, that after Mick Ronson, Bowie never shared the stage with anyone in quite the same way again. True, but Reeves must qualify as a partner who worked extremely closely and creatively with Bowie. I put this to Reeves:

> *I felt like that [that the pair was a partnership like Bowie and Ronson] and especially when he acknowledged my production input. With Hours in particular his analogy was that we were like Jagger/Richards. We wrote so much all the time. We would write different parts to songs, and if he got stuck I would come up with something, and if I got stuck he would come up with something. I mean, how do you acknowledge that? For the second Tin Machine album we split the publishing equally. Before we went onto record Hours, he said, "From now on, we'll put both names on everything."*

Another new addition to the team who would become a long-term collaborator, was multi-instrumentalist and producer Mark Plati, who joined for *Earthling*. His influence would be substantial as Bowie moved towards a new millennium.

Chapter 7
NEVER GET OLD

Programming, loops and samples. That was what Mark Plati was brought in to do for the *Earthling* album in 1996. Although in his earlier career, Bowie was known for assembling – dare I say, given the title of this book, collecting – bands, we have seen that, by the '90s, the musicians who joined him tended to stay; indeed, such was his commitment to his musicians, there were times when he ended up with three guitarists on stage. Nevertheless, he continued his propensity to absorb ideas and offer them, reborn, to the world, as he did with his partnership with Plati.

Mark remained with the band until 2003 and the album *Reality,* which seemed to announce Bowie's retirement but which turned out to be a decade-long hiatus. Having started with loops and samples, Plati added to his credits to the tune of acoustic and electric 12-string guitar, synth and drum programming, Mellotron, electric guitar, bass and keyboards. He was also the producer of *Earthling* and *Toy*. Bowie knew when he had a talent on his hands.

Mark's talent had already been proven many times over before he worked with Bowie. On his website he lists an impressive range of collaborations: "Between 1987 and

1991 Mark worked with such diverse artists as Quincy Jones, Janet Jackson, The Talking Heads, Fleetwood Mac, Lou Reed, Oingo Boingo, Dream Academy, The Fat Boys, Grayson Hugh, Pete Wylie, Dennis Brown, and the Bee Gees."

Plati settled down with Reeves Gabrels and Bowie to work on the album. Bowie had long been the master of nailing a vocal – and everything else – in a take or two but even so, because of Bowie's evident studio craft. He therefore tried to make sure he was recording most of the time – a process that was made easier by the fact that Plati was, unusually for this time, using a hard disk to capture everything. "Lucky for me, because the run-through guide vocal for 'Little Wonder' ended up being the only one he ever sang on that track! Most of the vocals were first take, which I had never seen before in my career."

'Battle for Britain (The Letter)' is the track that Mark Plati regards as "our first real Bowie song", adding, in conversation with David Buckley, that it was "an attempt to make a jazz-tinged jungle track," but that Bowie had reworked it, changing the chord structure.

Almost (but not quite) uniquely among Bowie writers, Chris O'Leary, in his second book of the songs of Bowie, *Ashes to Ashes*, describes the song musically as well as lyrically.

> *Bowie and Gabrels scrapped the original chord sequence, creating a new constellation of B major (verses), G major (pre-chorus) and C major (refrain) progressions. Plati thought 'The Letter' (its original title) got the album in focus – a sign that Bowie wanted strong melodic and harmonic structures so that Earthling would be actual songs over intense atmospheres.*

It fell to Plati to create the method of building the drum tracks that would give the album its manic jungle groove. Bowie was happy to use samples but only wanted to sample work they had created themselves. Plati had Zachary Alford create loops of various timings and sped them up from 120 to 160 bpm, and then had Alford improvise over the top of them, giving a manic, rampant quality.

It was this, more than anything, that gave the album what seems to me to be its defining feature – an exuberance so frenetic that it feels as though the band is constantly wrestling to harness it so that it doesn't run away with them. It was frenetic and certainly reminiscent of the jungle beats that were pervasive at the time but, due to the way it was built in-house, it was also distinct from its contemporaries.

As Gabrels said, in Paul Trynka's biography of Bowie, *Starman*, "it was nearly the twenty-first century and yet they were still playing like they were in the Rolling Stones," emphasising that he was still employing the perhaps outdated rock band format. Thus, he and Mark set about "making music out of bits of sonic 'junk' – old tracks or samples that he and Reeves found around the studio".

'Looking for Satellites' was the first conscious attempt to build something out of junk. It was also a conscious attempt by Plati to make an electronic track in waltz time. Again, David and Reeves scrapped the original chords.

There's no denying that a large factor in Bowie's longevity is his ability to make a perfectly timed tangential turn. By now, Bowie's reputation as an artist had been re-established with his recent three or four albums and his sales, while nowhere near the level of his mid '80s superstar success, were healthy. He was leading the way in experimental music and creating from scratch his own versions of drum and bass and jungle.

A new formula — and he didn't stick with it, of course.

As Hewitt puts it, "With three ingenious, artistically satisfying and commercially successful albums behind him [...] he went and wrote some songs".

The next album *Hours* brought further change. As far back as the '60s, Bowie and his contemporaries had been doing a thing they called "mixed media" – essentially taking a range of artistic disciplines such as painting, recording, poetry, mime and combining them to make a novel artistic form. The media of the new millennium was radically different in nature from that of 40 years earlier and Bowie was mixing it. On *Newsnight*, he had spoken to Jeremy Paxman about the huge potential for the internet to transform the artistic landscape and blur or obliterate the space between artist and consumer. Now Bowie started his own internet service provider, BowieNet, and participated fully, posting messages on its message board, releasing new music and giving behind the scenes access. He and Gabrels also wrote the music for the video game *Omikron: The Nomad Soul* – unconventionally producing 10 original songs rather than the moody atmospheric music that often accompanies games.

The songs from the game provided the musical direction and at times the source material for *Hours*.

Bowie and Gabrels initially recorded demos for the album in Bermuda. Bowie later explained that experimentation gave way to traditional song craft. The pair then went to the studio to record in earnest. Although Bowie's band had become quite settled and stable by now, only Mark Plati and Sterling Campbell returned – and even then not until halfway through the sessions. Indeed, Mark had heard rumours that Reeves and David were now working as a pair, sharing songwriting credits and recording between them. Reeves had wanted Plati to return from the off, but David resisted, perhaps seeing Mark as an experimenter and feeling that this album of conventional songs was a different beast.

At last, they got in touch to ask Plati to add some fretless bass to a song. A few hours' work turned into a few months. Becoming involved in production, he ended up mixing the album. He recalls the atmosphere as relaxed, with David, Reeves and himself swapping stories and laughing for hours.

Bowie, gatherer of talents and ideas, had found a route out of his commercially successful, artistically barren years with Reeves – but now that the task was done, others would walk the rest of the path with him. "Gabrels," says Paul Trynka, "prepared his own replacement" in Mark Plati.

Having completed the tour, David felt it would be a shame if the finely honed band didn't record an album. In another surprise move, he decided to make an album updating many of his pre-fame songs from the '60s and some originals.

The *Toy* album represents a distinctive chapter in his extensive discography, representing both a reflective look back at his early career and a fresh expression of his ever-evolving art. Recorded in 2000 but shelved until its eventual release in 2021, *Toy* stands out as a deeply personal project.

In *Toy*, Plati's role was multifaceted. He co-produced the album alongside Bowie, bringing his technical expertise and deep understanding of Bowie's artistic vision to the fore. Plati's production style, characterised by a blend of modern and retro elements, was crucial in giving the album its distinctive sound. The idea behind *Toy* was to capture the energy and spontaneity of a live performance while revisiting Bowie's early songs with a contemporary twist. Plati's production allowed the songs to breathe, maintaining their original charm while infusing them with a modern edge.

The recording sessions for *Toy* took place at New York's Sear Sound studio, where Plati worked closely with Bowie and the now stable group of trusted musicians, including guitarist Earl Slick, bassist Gail Ann Dorsey and drummer Sterling Campbell. Mike Garson also returned. Plati's role extended beyond production, of course. He also contributed as a musician, playing guitar and bass.

The album was scheduled for release but, claiming scheduling conflicts, Virgin delayed. And delayed. Publicly, Bowie claimed not to be bothered, saying that, as ever, he was more interested in the future. However, many biographers agree that he was quite hurt at the rejecting of this deeply personal album.

Eventually, the album was shelved, but *Toy* remained a fan favourite in bootleg form for years before its official release. When it finally saw the light of day in 2021, *Toy* was lauded for its raw energy and emotional depth, Plati's production receiving praise for capturing Bowie's vision.

Plati also introduced Bowie to Gerry Leonard, who was able to take the role of left-field experimental guitarist previously played by the likes of Fripp, Belew and Gabrels. I was fortunate to interview Gerry at length for *David Bowie Glamour* in 2018.

It was a spirit of experimentation that brought Gerry's skills, through Plati, to the attention of David Bowie. Gerry remembers that he was working in the B room of Philip Glass's Looking Glass studios in New York while David and

Mark were in the A room. Having worked with Gerry on a number of previous occasions, Plati took one of Bowie's tracks to Gerry because "he had this idea that he would have me do my kind of ambient guitar thing that I was making my reputation on." Clearly, the result was well received because Gerry was then invited to meet David and ended up playing on a number of other tracks from the sessions. Asked which tracks he contributed to, Gerry confirms that 'Uncle Floyd' (later to emerge as 'Slip Away') and 'Shadow Man' were among them. David, according to Gerry, was much enamoured with American comedian Floyd Vivino's character of Uncle Floyd at that time.

"David had all these songs that he'd either put on the back burner or he wanted to remake," he explains – and that his thoughts were turning more towards live performance. "It came out in the end on the *Heathen* and *Reality* records 'cos we could play that stuff live. David wasn't afraid to start over. I think when he did the *Heathen* record it was a very different record than the *Toy* record. So, I think that was a one-eighty. He just kind of decided, 'Okay, I'm going to do something else,' so by the time we got to do the *Reality* tour I think he was thinking of what the live show would be, so the *Reality* record was written towards touring."

Famously, at Gerry's first gig with David Bowie, the band played the *Heathen* and *Low* albums in their entirety. "It was daunting," he reveals, but quickly adds, "It was interesting. So I had this initial meeting with David through Mark where I got to play on some stuff and then I think what happened was, David decided he was going to do the Meltdown festival in London and for that he was going to do the *Heathen* record which was his new album at the time, and the *Low* record and compare the two and so then they considered me as one of the guitar players because I could offer more of the 'out of the box' stuff than the Robert Fripps and the Enos could offer. It was the crossing over thing. So, he came down and saw one of my solo shows. He saw a Spooky Ghost show and I think his question to Mark was, 'Can Gerry rock?' And I guess we did rock that night! It was *very* daunting to have him there, I can tell you. I was a nervous wreck! But then, on the back of that, he asked me to join the band and we started working on the stuff."

This led to a partnership during which Gerry worked on the *Heathen* album and tour and then the *Reality* album and its tour, on which he served as musical director. The *Reality* tour ended abruptly but seemed to have been a pretty joyful time up till that point.

"It was pretty extraordinary," Gerry confirms. "David had just come back to playing live. He did the Glastonbury headliner with Mark as MD and that kind of kickstarted the thing where he was doing the *Toy* record, and he was doing the *Heathen* record and he was doing the *Reality* record and by then he had these big plans for the *Reality* tour. That was the biggest tour he's done, I think, in a long time, so… it was an amazing experience, that tour. We had a really great band. He was really on good form and really ready to do these two-and-a-half hour, three-hour shows and he just wanted to work so I remember it as being a really busy period."

The role of musical director is truly an onerous one and, to a large extent, the success of the tour depends on the creative decisions they make. Gerry explains how the role came to him: "Mark Plati had to go on to another project and was unable to be the MD for the tour and that got passed over to me because I was friends with Mark and

I had some background in recording." The pace, evidently, was frantic. "Starting all the pre-production. Being on the phone. Talking to David. Getting it all together and then, just even that initial process of getting a huge amount of material together and doing all the pre-production and starting to work with visuals David was doing."

He continues, "Working with the lighting people and visuals and then we started doing the touring and also promoting this *Reality* record, so it was in-*sane*! Then we got into the tour proper and I can remember us having four days off and then heading back out!" It seems there was great pressure on Gerry, but the phenomenal critical and commercial success of the tour shows that he carried the task out with aplomb. At least once the tour itself began he could surely relax and just concentrate on being a guitar player, couldn't he? Not really.

"David kept wanting to do new songs. He would say, you know, 'Dylan's got 84 songs. Let's keep doing songs.' We had 64 songs in our songbook. We would work them up at soundcheck and try new arrangements. It was a really dynamic time." Although it was exhausting, he adds that, "David was such a great artist, it was an absolute pleasure to put in the long days and see the results from it."

By this stage of his career, David was comfortable with his past and had laid his characters and alter egos to rest. "It *was* David Bowie. It took down the veil. Even the way he interacted with the crowd."

A partnership that had started with Mark Plati and the *Toy* album prospered and endured. At the same time, another partnership was rekindled. Towards the end of the making of *Toy*, Tony Visconti was brought in to score a string arrangement. Way back in the '60s, it was Tony who had advocated for the recruitment of a stable band. Now, the band was indeed not only solid and stable but also artistically creative and innovative. The final piece in that jigsaw to complete the properly stable team was to be Visconti himself.

* * *

Tony Visconti's collaboration with David Bowie on the albums *Heathen* and *Reality* marked a significant reunion between the pair. Having worked together since the late 1960s, Visconti and Bowie's partnership produced some of the most influential albums in rock history. *Heathen*, released in 2002, was Bowie's 23rd studio album and marked his first collaboration with Visconti on a full album in over 20 years. The album emerged at a time when Bowie was reflecting on his legacy and the state of the world. Its lyrics are often read as a reflection on the September 11 attacks but were in fact written before. *Heathen* is filled with a sense of melancholy, introspection and a deep awareness of mortality.

As co-producer, Visconti was central to the sonic character of *Heathen*. The production is lush and layered, blending electronic textures with organic instrumentation. Visconti's orchestral arrangements, particularly on the tracks 'Sunday' and 'I Would Be Your Slave,' add a grand, almost cinematic quality to the album, while his careful attention to detail ensured that every element of the soundscape contributed to the album's themes.

Building on the success of Heathen, Bowie and Visconti quickly returned to the studio to create Reality, released in 2003. While Heathen was introspective and sombre, Reality took on a more outward-looking and assertive tone.

Visconti's production on *Reality* was more stripped down compared to the lushness of *Heathen*, but no less impactful. The album has a raw, live feel, with a rock-oriented sound that harkened back to Bowie's earlier work while still feeling fresh and relevant. Tony's approach allowed Bowie's vocals and lyrics to take centre stage, with the instrumentation providing a powerful, driving force behind them. As Tony once told me, "David and I just got better at what we do."

Both *Heathen* and *Reality* were critically acclaimed and commercially successful. Bowie's status as a major artist and innovator had long been reasserted but these albums offered reinforcement. For Tony Visconti, these albums were a testament to his long-standing partnership with Bowie and to an enduring friendship.

The team was complete. The tour, a triumph. The band, as Gerry Leonard confirmed, had a repertoire of over 60 songs to choose from. David was on top form. He appeared relaxed and youthful. "Ageing," he said, "is an extraordinary process whereby you become the person you always should have been."

On 23 June 2004, during a show in Prague, Bowie left the stage, clearly in some pain. The band played two numbers without him before Bowie returned for a few numbers and left again before returning once more. A trapped nerve was suspected and diagnosed. Bowie played a concert two days later in Scheessel, Germany. Recordings show a clearly depleted Bowie nevertheless turning in an astonishing performance. Let me encourage you to search online for his performance of '"Heroes"'.

After the show, Bowie was in a great deal of pain and was rushed to Hamburg's St George Hospital where he was found to be suffering from a blocked artery. He underwent an angioplasty – a procedure in which a tube is inserted into the artery in order to maintain the flow of blood. The tour was over but, even truncated, had been a huge success.

After this, we heard from Bowie only sporadically for the next 10 years. Musically, he appeared with Mike Garson at an event called Fashion Rocks to perform 'Life on Mars?' and later 'Five Years' alongside Arcade Fire. The following year he surprised everyone by appearing alongside David Gilmour at the Royal Albert Hall to perform 'Arnold Layne' and the doctor part on 'Comfortably Numb'. Then, in 2006, he performed three songs, two alongside Alicia Keys, at the Black Ball benefit event, organised by Iman. He also made a few screen appearances, playing a fictionalised version of the inventor Nikola Tesla in Christopher Nolan's film *The Prestige* and as himself in the TV television series *Extras*, in a hilarious performance alongside Ricky Gervais.

Bowie did not disappear or withdraw from the public gaze, as some would have it, but he scaled back his workload massively. It appeared he was now largely retired and would not work on new music again. He was focused on family life. Who could blame him?

But of course, Bowie liked to surprise us.

* * *

I recall turning on breakfast TV on the morning of 8 January 2013 – Bowie's 66th birthday - and seeing, through bleary eyes, that there was talk of Bowie. It became clear, as I pulled myself together and listened more that Bowie had released a single. This was out of the blue, to say the least! It seemed Bowie had been in the studio in secret. All the band had signed NDAs, as had producer Tony Visconti. An album was recorded too, and was set for release.

With its reflective lyrics and sombre tone, 'Where Are We Now?' captures Bowie looking back on his time in Berlin during the late 1970s, a period that profoundly influenced his work on the albums *Low* and *"Heroes"*.

The song's melancholy melody, balancing with Bowie's fragile vocal delivery, creates a sense of nostalgia and introspection. Lyrically, Bowie references specific locations in Berlin, such as the Bösebrücke and the Dschungel nightclub, which hold personal significance from his time living in the city. The repeated question: *Where are we now?* is a poignant reflection on time, change, and memory.

The album followed exactly two months later. *The Next Day* surprised fans and critics alike, both for its sudden arrival and its content, which seemed to seamlessly blend Bowie's classic sound with contemporary themes.

The album's cover art, a defaced version of Bowie's iconic *"Heroes"* album, sets the tone for the music within – an artist revisiting his past while simultaneously forging ahead. *The Next Day* is a bold, dynamic record that draws heavily from Bowie's rich history, particularly his Berlin Trilogy era, while addressing themes of mortality, ageing and the passage of time. Yet, it is far from a nostalgic retread; instead, it is a statement of reinvention and resilience.

Musically, *The Next Day* is diverse, spanning genres from rock to art pop. The title track and 'Valentine's Day' showcase Bowie's rock sensibilities with driving rhythms and sharp lyrics, while 'Where Are We Now?' offers a more introspective, melancholic reflection on his time in Berlin. 'Love Is Lost' and 'The Stars (Are Out Tonight)' explore darker, more complex emotional territories, with Bowie's voice conveying both vulnerability and power.

Lyrically, the album is rich with imagery and layered

meanings, often addressing Bowie's own legacy and the complexities of fame. 'I'd Rather Be High' delves into themes of disillusionment and the burden of the past, while others, such as 'How Does the Grass Grow?' and 'You Will Set the World on Fire,' offer sharp social and political commentary. Overall, the album is reflective, and Tony Visconti commented that in the studio they had listened only to Bowie albums co-produced by Tony*: Lodger*, *Scary Monsters*, *Heathen*. Although the album was intended to be something new, "something old kept creeping in".

> The Next Day *was met with widespread critical acclaim, praised for its vitality and Bowie's ability to remain relevant and innovative even in his later years. It was also a commercial success, reaching the top spot in the UK and number 2 in the USA.*

With the notable exception of Mark Plati, the band that Bowie had assembled over the previous years all returned. Zack Alford played drums on almost all of the 14 tracks (17 if we include the expanded edition, *The Next Day Extra*). Sterling Campbell played on two and was disappointed not to have been contacted, initially. He told me:

> The Next Day *– I did take it a little badly [that] I wasn't doing as much. But the fact he still called me back in was like,* OK. *[dreamy voice]* He still likes me! *David, he's on that level. He's a one-off. It's the one and only time that's gonna happen. There's only one Mozart. Only one Liszt.*

Bowie had surprised us all. 'Twas ever thus.
He had one more surprise for us.

Chapter 8
I CAN'T GIVE EVERYTHING AWAY

On 8 January 2016 – once again, his birthday – Bowie released his new album, *Blackstar*. On the 10th, he died. There had been no public hint that he had been ill and every indication that his health concerns of the previous decade were resolved. It has been widely reported that he had been suffering from liver cancer, diagnosed eighteen months before his passing.

Masterpiece though it is, the album remains a painful listen for many, entwined as it is with his passing.

In June 2014, Bowie worked up some demos with Tony and Zachary Alford. Also in June, Bowie had seen a jazz band, led by Donny McCaslin, play in the 55 Bar in the West Village of Manhattan. Donny kindly did an in-depth interview for our fifth issue of the fanzine. He said:

> *The real story is that Bowie was working on 'Sue' [a single Bowie had released after* The Next Day *but prior to* Blackstar*] with Maria Schneider. I was in her band. They were talking about the rhythmic underpinning of 'Sue' and Maria said, 'Let me play you something, David.' She played him one of my records and evidently suggested that*

he do something with me and my group. That's really what started it. If I remember correctly, Maria suggested a couple more times that David work with me. Then it happened that David saw that we were going to be playing at the 55 Club and reached out to Maria about the gig. Maria suggested they come and see us play. It was at the time we were about to attend the first workshop about the Maria collaboration on 'Sue'.

I saw David out of the corner of my eye during the gig and I tried not to think about it. It was a tune up gig before a recording I was going to do ('Fast Future'), so I had a lot of stuff going on in my mind. Then they were gone! I didn't see him after the gig and I didn't meet him then. About a week later I went to the first 'Sue' rehearsal and David was there. That's when we first met. Tony Visconti was there as were my band.

So impressed was Bowie that he decided this was the band he wanted to work with. Before doing so, he sent messages to his regular band that he was doing something but "not to worry," which Gerry Leonard said in conversation with me that he took to mean he would be working with his usual band again in the future.

In the studio, Donny recalls that he could feel the history between the two old friends, David and Tony. "Tony knew what to do with David right away. Tony instructed the engineer how to deal with David's vocal overdubs and it was seamless." There was no indication as far as Donny could see that Bowie was ill. "He was OK," he says. "It's hard to know. I hadn't known him long and had no point of reference. His energy was great, and he was talking on point. He was very sharp indeed."

The album, when released, hit number one in most territories, no doubt partly because of the news of his death. The album's reception was overwhelmingly positive. *Rolling Stone* called it "a ricochet of textural eccentricity and pictorial-shrapnel writing', whereas the *Daily Telegraph* called it an "extraordinary" album which "suggests that, like a modern-day Lazarus of pop, Bowie is well and truly back from beyond."

What is remarkable, as Nicholas Pegg notes in the indispensable *The Complete David Bowie*, is that in the couple of short days following the album's release but before Bowie's death was reported, no reviewer of the album remarked upon the one thing that now seems so glaringly obvious – the many references to death. Yet there it was in front of us: "Look up here, I'm in heaven", "Something happened on the day he died", "On the day of execution" and "I'm dying to" are among the more unequivocal references. Meaning can be read into many more: "I know something's very wrong", "The Blackout harks with flowered muse", "If I'll never see the English evergreens", "I've got nothing left to lose".

It's tempting to say that the two days that we were afforded for analysis before his passing was insufficient time to see these clues. However, four of the album's seven tracks had been released well prior to the appearance of the final album. 'Blackstar' had been released as a single in November 2015 and was used as the opening music for the television series, *The Last Panthers*. The single was followed by 'Lazarus' in December. Prior to both of these, both 'Sue (or In a Season of Crime)' and ''Tis a Pity She Was a Whore' had been released in a different form. There was ample opportunity to analyse the lyrics – and yet the motif of death was missed.

Perhaps for good reason. In his well-considered and astute book *Why Bowie Matters*, Will Brooker notes that many of Bowie's albums may be interpreted as a treatise on death. Cut and paste *Aladdin Sane* into *Blackstar's* place and it is very possible to read the lyrical content as the last testament of a dying man. "Paris or maybe hell (I'm waiting)", "She will be your living end", "A gun and me alone", "You're knocking me dead". Add to this the musing on death as puppet-master in 'Time' and it begins to emerge that *Blackstar* is not the only one of Bowie's albums to be profoundly concerned with our shared and inevitable fates. Any of a number of his other works could fill the role admirably. *Hunky Dory* ("He could be dead, he could be not, he could be you", "Knowledge comes with death's release") would be a fine candidate. *Diamond Dogs* would do the job superbly ("And in the death", "We are the dead"). Others, such as *Heathen*, *The Man Who Sold the World* and many more would perform the role just as well.

It is tempting, then, to see *Blackstar* not as Bowie's final musing or last message but as simply another album with a familiar subject matter imbued with meaning by its listeners as a result of its unfortunate timing. And yet Alexis Petridris, writing in the *Guardian*, commented on the traditional inscrutability of Bowie's lyrics, noting that 'I Can't Give Everything Away', the album's closing track, seems to be Bowie's wry comment of "best of luck with that" to those attempting to unravel his lyrics. "Saying no but meaning yes, this is all I ever meant." Bowie's words have always been available for multiple interpretations. This is what marks him out as an artist rather than simply an entertainer.

There are, however, two reasons to separate *Blackstar* from Bowie's other work on the subject. First is the very fact of its lineage as the final instalment in a career-long thematic preoccupation with the subject and the second is its unique treatment of the subject of death.

This is perhaps the great difference between *Blackstar* and its predecessor albums. One could not simply replace *Blackstar* with *Aladdin Sane* at the end of Bowie's career and imbue that earlier album with the significance of *Blackstar*. Despite the significant similarity of the shared theme of death and time, there is a crucial difference, noted by Pegg: "the howling anguish has gone". Nowhere in *Blackstar* do we see the desperate pleas for more time ("I had so many dreams") or the hopeful bargaining of the relentless pursuit and escape ("You are not a victim"). In its place we find the peaceful reflection of a man looking back on his life – a very different viewpoint from that of a young man looking forward towards his own death.

The swirling, unhurried, joyous melodies and harmonies of 'Blackstar' establish the new-found serenity and complement the many lyrical indications of acceptance: "Something happened on the day he died. / Spirit rose a metre and stepped aside", "Just go with me", "Oh, I'll be free. / Just like that bluebird."

The young man full of life is concerned with matters of death whereas the older man, closer to death, is concerned with reflections on life.

* * *

When David Bowie was working with an ever-changing cast of characters, Tony Visconti had known that what Bowie needed was a stable band. Both Visconti and Bowie worked hard to achieve that and David had success with the Spiders from Mars, the D.A.M. Trio, Tin Machine, and the

Reality era band. Tony's view was vindicated. In the final decades of his career, Bowie truly achieved the stability he needed with an expert but inspirational group of musicians.

And yet, for his final album, the two remaining components were simply Bowie and Visconti himself. It is they who were the solid, stable unit.

ABOUT THE AUTHOR

Nick Smart is joint editor and designer of the popular fanzine, *David Bowie Glamour*. He has been a fan of David Bowie since 1979 and has interviewed and written articles on many of Bowie's collaborators. He jointly curated the David Bowie World Fan Convention in Liverpool, 2022 and New York 2023 and through his Fanzine and Convention has created a substantial following of Bowie fans on social media. He holds a master's degree in English, has three grown up children and lives in Somerset with his wife, Kathrine.

www.nicksmart.net

ACKNOWLEDGEMENTS

In my other life, I'm a teacher. If, as they say, it takes a village to educate a child, then it takes a city to write a book.

Andy Jones, my uncle and my partner in the fanzine and conventions, was my introduction to Bowie. It was he who gave me records, told me about Bowie, took me to concerts and generally immersed me in Bowie. Thanks, And.

I offer my warm thanks to my very good friend Nicholas Pegg. The conversations we have had about Bowie have been illuminating and inspiring, as have all the other conversations. His book *The Complete David Bowie* is indispensable for any Bowie fan and has been indispensable for me while writing this book. His Bowie knowledge is encyclopaedic and unsurpassed and his prose is beautiful. This book has benefited enormously from his fact-checking and of course, his Foreword. I'd like to thank my good friend Barnaby Edwards most sincerely and warmly, too.

I'd also like to thank David Buckley, author of the definitive biography *Strange Fascination*, for the many insights and facts contained therein. Much of what we know about Bowie was uncovered by him.

Although much of what is contained in these pages comes from interviews Andy and I have conducted, much also comes from the work of others before us. In addition to those mentioned above, I'd like to gratefully mention Chris O'Leary, Paolo Hewitt, Kevin Cann, Will Brooker, Paul Trynka, Tom Hagler and Dylan Jones for their excellent books, all of which have been piled up around me for months (in fact, years, on and off) while I have been writing this book.

For his extraordinary generosity, I thank Philippe Auliac, master photographer who photographed Bowie over many years and has allowed lots of them to be reproduced here, including the cover image. I am honoured to have them on the cover and in these pages and the book is the richer for them.

My sincere gratitude also to Chris Duffy and Sandie Goodman at the Duffy Archive for the use of such iconic images. They are fabulous and I'm delighted to have been able to reproduce them here.

Also, David Currie for very kindly sharing his fabulous photography and insights just when I was beginning to despair.

Mark Adams has been thoughtful and just great on this journey. For their support, my gratitude to Paul Kinder, who runs the amazing Bowie Wonderworld site and media and has supported this journey and put the word out. Thank you also to Nick Vernon of David Bowie News for his support from the start.

Christine O'Growney, John Brereton and others run the amazing Dublin Bowie Festival and their generous advice has been a great support to us. Likewise, Liz Cooper and Francesca Shashkova who run the annual London Bowie Event for the Terrence Higgins Trust, which is a wonderful occasion for a great cause.

I also owe a huge debt of gratitude to everyone who has contributed to the magazine over its lifetime. David Bowie's associates, friends and collaborators have been enormously generous with their time and willingness to share. They say you can tell a man by the company he keeps, and David Bowie clearly chose his well. Thanks too to everyone who sent a story, photo, artwork, poem or anything else.

The Bowie tribe is strong, and I'd like to express my thanks to all those I meet at Bowie events and have become friends with, including Gillian, Janine, Janine, Beth, Ian, Jim, Shan, Ersula, Sonia, Lisa and Charlie.

Thank you, Marc Andrews and Rebel Heroes, and thank you, Charlie Fowler and David Live. You lift any Bowie occasion with your amazing musical homages to Bowie. Likewise, the aforementioned John Brereton and The London Boys.

I'd like to say thank you to Kate Amor for being interested and for all her advice. Yes, you can be my agent!

Thank you to my friend Garry Wilde for the endless hours of strumming and playing Bowie songs interspersed with good conversations. Thanks too, to my old friend Doug Thrower for the hours and decades of music. I think we may be ready! And thank you to Jon Pullen for his friendship, sage publishing advice and the opportunity to make like the boy in the bright blue jeans.

Our libraries are under great threat these days. Many libraries, whether they knew it or not, have helped sustain this book, including Weston-super-Mare Central Library and the Campus Library in Weston. Also, Bath Spa University Library and many others.

Tabitha Palmer who designed the cover of this book from Philippe's photo. Thank you.

Caroline and Andy Peden Smith, my fabulous publishers. Thank you for believing in this book and giving it time to flourish, thank you for squeezing your work into such a short period of time because my work had expanded into a longer period, and thank you for saving me from *Homes Under the Hammer*.

Warm thanks to my mum who has been writing her book alongside mine. We have shared a journey. Thank you for everything, mum.

My brothers, Dave and Steve Smart, are my greatest mates. The gigs we attend together are special to me and to both of you, I know.

Sophie, Josh and Sky, my children. You are amazing. I'm so proud of each of you and I love you more than anything.

Kathrine, my love. Forty years of devotion. This book couldn't have been finished without your support. Thank you for waking me at 6.00 a.m. because you knew the only way I'd get it done was to get a couple of hours in before work. Thank you for sacrificing your only two weeks' holiday this year so that I could finish my final push. Thank you for being there through illness and everything else.

And thank you, dear reader, for being interested.

BIBLIOGRAPHY

Allred, Mike, et al. *Bowie: Stardust, Rayguns & Moonage Daydreams*. Insight Comics, 2020.

Aris, Brian. *Memories of Bowie*. Snap Galleries, 2020.

Armstrong, Kevin. *Absolute Beginner*. Jawbone Press, 2023.

Bell, Edward. *Unmade up : Recollections of a Friendship with David Bowie*. Unicorn, 2017.

Bowie, David, and Tom Hagler. *Bowie at the BBC*. Welbeck, 2023.

Bowie, David, and Grant London. *Pocket Bowie Wisdom*. Hardie Grant Books, 2016.

Broackes, Victoria, et al. *David Bowie Is the Subject*. V & A Publishing, 2013.

Brooker, Will. *Forever Stardust*. Bloomsbury Publishing, 2017.

——. *Why Bowie Matters*. HarperCollins UK, 2019.

Buckley, David. *Strange Fascination: David Bowie, the Definitive Story*. Virgin Books, 2016.

Cambridge, John. *Bowie, Cambridge & All the Hype*. McNidder & Grace, 2021.

Cann, Kevin. *Any Day Now: David Bowie: The London Years, 1947–1974*. Adelita, 2010.

Cann, Kevin, and Chris Duffy. *Duffy Bowie*. ACC Editions, 2019.

Cinque, Toija, et al. *Enchanting David Bowie: Space/Time/Body/Memory*. Bloomsbury Academic, 2015.

Creed, Rupert, and Garry Burnett. *The Mick Ronson Story*. McNidder & Grace, 2022.

Critchley, Simon. *On Bowie*. Serpent's Tail, 2016.

Cummins, Kevin. *David Bowie: Mixing Memory and Desire*. Weldon Owen International, 2023.

Currie, David. *David Bowie: Glass Idol.* Omnibus Press, 1987.

Currie, David, and Kevin Cann. *David Bowie.* Omnibus Press, 1985.

Devereux, Eoin, et al. *David Bowie.* Routledge, 2015.

Doggett, Peter. *The Man Who Sold the World: David Bowie and the 1970s.* Harperperennial, 2013.

Duffy, Chris. *Aladdin Sane 50.* Welbeck, 2023.

Egan, Sean, and David Bowie. *Bowie on Bowie: Interviews and Encounters with David Bowie.* Chicago Review Press, 2015.

Evans, Mike, and David Bowie. *Bowie Treasures.* Carlton Books, 2016.

Fletcher, David Jeffrey. *David Robert Jones Bowie: The Discography of a Generalist, 1962–1979.* F. Fergeson Productions, 1979.

Gilbert, Pat. *Bowie: The Illustrated Story.* Voyageur Press, 2017.

Gillman, Peter, and Leni Gillman. *Alias David Bowie.* Henry Holt, 1987.

Goddard, Simon. *Bowie Odyssey 70.* Omnibus Press, 2020.

——. *Bowie Odyssey 71.* Omnibus Press, 2021.

——. *Bowie Odyssey 73.* Omnibus Press, 2023.

——. *Bowie Odyssey 74.* Omnibus Press, 2024.

Griffin, Roger. *David Bowie: The Golden Years.* Omnibus Press, 2016.

Hagler, Tom. *We Could Be.* Hachette UK, 2021.

Heller, Jason. *Strange Stars.* Melville House, 2018.

Hewitt, Paolo. *David Bowie: Album by Album.* Carlton Books Ltd, 2013.

Isabel Sanchez Vegara. *Little People, Big Dreams – David Bowie.* Frances Lincoln Children's Books, 2019.

Jérôme Soligny. *David Bowie Rainbowman.* Monoray, 2023.

Jones, Dylan. *David Bowie: A Life.* Éditions Ring, 2018.

——. *When Ziggy Played Guitar.* Random House, 2012.

Kardos, Leah. *Blackstar Theory.* Bloomsbury Publishing USA, 2021.

Lancaster, Phil. *At the Birth of Bowie: Life with the Man Who Became a Legend.* John Blake, 2019.

Leigh, Wendy. *Bowie.* Editora Best Seller, 2016.

MacCormack, Geoff. *David Bowie: Rock 'N' Roll with Me.* Acc Art Books, 2023.

Mayes, Sean. *Life on Tour with Bowie.* Music Press Books, 2016.

Mick Rock, et al. *Moonage Daydream: The Life and Times of Ziggy Stardust.* Schwarzkopf & Schwarzkopf, 2006.

Morley, Paul. *Age of Bowie*. Simon & Schuster, 2014.
O'Leary, Chris. *Ashes to Ashes*. Watkins Media Limited, 2019.
——. *Rebel Rebel*. John Hunt Publishing, 2015.
O'Neill, Terry. *Bowie by O'Neill*. Cassell, 2019.
O'Regan, Denis, et al. *Ricochet: David Bowie 1983: An Intimate Portrait*. Particular Books, 2018.
Paytress, Mark, and Steve Pafford. *Bowiestyle*. Omnibus, 2016.
Pegg, Nicholas. *The Complete David Bowie (Revised and Updated 2016 Edition)*. Titan Books, 2016.
Rachel, Daniel, and Carrie Kania. *David Bowie: Icon*. Iconic Images, 2020.
Royle, Nicholas. *David Bowie, Enid Blyton and the Sun Machine*. Manchester University Press, 2023.
Slick, Earl. *Guitar*. Michael Joseph, 2025.
Spitz, Marc. *Bowie*. Klim, 2016.
Steiner, Adam. *Silhouettes and Shadows*. Backbeat Books, 2023.
Thomson, Elizabeth, and David Gutman. *The Bowie Companion*. Da Capo Press, 1996.
Trynka, Paul. *Starman: David Bowie : The Definitive Biography*. Sphere, 2012.
Visconti, Tony. *Tony Visconti: The Autobiography: Bowie, Bolan and the Brooklyn Boy*. HarperCollins UK, 2009.
Wardell, Mark, and Susan Compo. *The Fly in the Milk: David Bowie*. Red Planet Books, 2023.
Weird & Gilly. *Mick Ronson – the Spider with the Platinum Hair*. Bonnier Zaffre, 2017.
Wide, Steve. *Bowie A to Z*. National Geographic Books, 2016.
Woodmansey, Woody, et al. *Spider from Mars*. Sidgwick & Jackson, 2016.
Zanetta, Tony, and Henry Edwards. *Stardust*. Michael Joseph, 1986.

Websites

"David Bowie." *David Bowie*, www.davidbowie.com.
Kinder, Paul. "David Bowie Wonderworld." www.bowiewonderworld.com.
O'Leary, Chris. "Pushing ahead of the Dame." *Pushing ahead of the Dame*, bowiesongs.wordpress.com.

"The Ziggy Stardust Companion - a David Bowie Website.", 2015, 5years.com.

Vernon, Nick. "David Bowie News | Celebrating the Genius of David Bowie." *David Bowie News*, www.davidbowienews.com.

INDEX